life
eclipses
death

A MOTHER AND DAUGHTER'S ILLUMINATING JOURNEY
TO FIND JOY IN LIFE AND PEACE WITH DEATH

life
eclipses
death

LIZ VANCE & DIANA BEE STEFFEN

Life Eclipses Death: A mother and daughter's illuminating journey to find joy in life and peace with death

For information about this title or to order other books and/ or electronic media, contact the publisher:

Liz Vance
theawakeself.com
intuitiveliz@yahoo.com

ISBNs:
978-1-7364610-0-6 (print)
979-1-7364610-1-3 (eBook)

Printed in the United States of America

Cover and Interior design: 1106 Design

This book is dedicated to my family,
both of birth and of choice. Your support and compassion brought me
through the toughest times with grace.

Contents

A Note from the Author

When I finished writing this book and sent it to my editor in March 2020, the coronavirus, a life-threatening and highly contagious disease, entered into the world. Humanity was faced with a global pandemic, and death and dying became a part of our daily news.

I have been a practicing intuitive healer for twenty-five years. People call on me when they are going through challenges in their lives. We explore relationships, death, divorce, job changes, anger issues, grief, life purpose, and much more. I connect with them through my intuition and give them guidance based on what I see and feel. Throughout my career, I have helped people process grief and serious illness.

The coronavirus required everyone across the United States and the world to collectively face the possibility of dying and losing people they love. Since March, I have been working with clients who have lost parents, friends, co-workers, and family members. The whole world woke up to the realization that life is precious and that each moment shared is a gift.

This realization was not new to me. When I was in my early forties, my mom was diagnosed with terminal cancer. She had always been my best friend and my heart dropped when I heard the news. Due to the nature of my work, I felt like I had been in training all of my life to be able to walk through her treatment and eventually her passing, but what I knew was challenged to the depth of my soul, and I failed as much as I succeeded along the way.

What I discovered from my personal experience with death and dying was that no matter how much I gave guidance to people going through the loss of someone close to them, there was nothing that compared to going through the process myself. Accompanying Mom through her journey with cancer was a humbling and eye-opening experience.

Mom's journey was both heartbreaking and inspiring. One did not negate the other. As much as I know that there is a divine part of us that never dies, the human part of me had to bear witness to the dying process and eventual death of my mom.

Mom's life, especially at the end of her life, transformed me. May the story of my beautiful mom Diana Bee Steffen bring strength, inspiration, and love to all who need it.

Chapter One

Raccoons

The fated moment was here. My mom—my best friend, my confidant—died.

For a time, the sun stopped shining, the world stopped spinning, and I felt incredibly alone.

My heart aches from the loss. But equal to the ache is the inspiration and joy she infused in my life. This was especially true after she was diagnosed with cancer and decided to face her final days with strength and spirit.

She could have just let go, but instead she was inspired to live.

The years that led to the moment when she passed away were filled with powerful experiences that woke her up to life. She woke up and everyone around her woke up, either for a moment or for a lifetime.

I was lucky to be one who was changed for a lifetime.

As I cleared out Mom's things after she died, I found her writing scattered among everything she owned. I cannot share this journey without having her words alongside mine.

She was always working on ideas, most of them short and fun to read. She wrote,

> She had a kernel of a memory of herself as a young girl having an idea and eagerly writing it down.

Stories were at the essence of Mom. She was a lyrical woman with an animated personality, and she dressed with flair and style. In conversations, she leapt at the chance to weave images of worlds, places, and events that would invoke a new way of thinking.

She inherited her love of storytelling from her father, who I remember as a tall man with a continual grin on his face. His fishing cap sat crookedly on his head, and he was always ready to spin a good narrative. He passed along the love of a small tale or a tall tale, or any kind of tale one could tell. Mom wrote a story about him.

> It seemed as if Dad had just left the house to go to school and he was back home. And, as my grandfather used to say, he had a "shit-eating grin on his face."
>
> "You won't believe what I've found," he said.
>
> And what should it be but five baby raccoons, all skittering and scattering around the back of his Woodie station wagon like the playful babies that they were.
>
> My sister and I actually screeched when we saw them.
>
> "Where did you find them?" we asked.
>
> "You wouldn't believe it! Right in the middle of Layton Avenue," said my dad, referring to the busy highway in front of our house.
>
> "Noooo!" said my sister, elongating the word to show her disbelief.

Dad explained that he had been driving up the hill and he noticed some small animals in the road. He stopped and saw that they were baby raccoons. Their mother had been killed on the highway and three of the babies were gathered by her, mewing as loud as could be. One had its head raised up with the pain of losing its mom, another one was licking its mom's tail over and over again, and the other two had wandered off in different directions.

"I got an old gunny sack out of the trunk and somehow got them all in it and as you can see, they escaped all over the car," Dad said.

Every raccoon responded differently to the loss. Some stayed present and mourned, and some wandered off in shock. In essence, we all deal with loss differently like those baby raccoons, and the loss of a mother runs deep inside of us.

Mom had a lot of incredible relationships in her life and each person, just like each raccoon, had their own connection with her and their own way of mourning. My brother Mike, my aunt Betty, and I were all equally Mom's people. This story is from my perspective, and they each have their own amazing tales of Mom to tell.

Mom wanted her stories to be told, and she always said that writing was her middle name.

I was meant to be a writer from a very young age. When I was three or four years old, my mom gave me one of her big black purses and a big pad of paper. I would sit for hours in my parents' 1936 Chevy in the back seat and I would "write." It was just scribbles, but I had ideas about what I was trying to say.

Mom gave me a notebook to write in when I was little as well. When I was in second grade, she gave me the assignment to write a page a day. My first page was, "I am very, very, very, very, very . . . very {to the end of the page} happy." She was very, very, very proud and encouraged me to add some extra words. It took me awhile, but eventually my journal writing became more and more detailed.

She was an English teacher and would bring me to her journalism classes at the local community college. I was eight and I felt so grown-up to be sitting in a college class. Her students always treated me like an adult, and I would sit with rapt attention as my mom engaged the students with talk about choosing words and ideas. It was always interesting to hear her encouraging people to find their story in the different aspects of life that they encountered. Sometimes the story seemed obvious, but the nuances were always unique to the writer, and Mom encouraged that uniqueness in herself and others.

Mom was also a dancer—a ballerina—and I remember her role as the Wicked Witch in a local production of *The Wizard of Oz*. Her face was painted green, she wore a flowing black dress, and her expressive movements embodied the character. She was so engaging and entertaining that she stole the show!

She wrote reviews in the local paper for all the dance companies that came through town, and the two of us would dress up and head to the shows together. As she drove me home after the performance, we would talk over what she would write. We would have dynamic discussions on whether or not we liked the dances and the engaging words she could use to describe the dancers. She would drop me off at the house and then head to the paper to finish her article by the midnight deadline.

Mom was always working on a novel, although the novel was never the same one. She had curiosity and liked to explore so many different worlds in her mind. She would plan out a book and then a new idea would come to her and distract her from the one before. Her projects were ever evolving, and she created more than her share of stories that were never finished.

At the end of her life, she was working on a novel that expressed Mom's essential nature. It was a semi-autobiographical tale of a journey she took when she was fifteen with her sister and a few young friends. She was a revolutionary, an adventurer, and someone who was brave, courageous, and fun. She was not arrogant and did not speak of these traits; she just embodied them in everything she did. She expressed this in the beginning chapter of her novel.

We were about to board a Greyhound bus in Milwaukee and travel 1,100 miles to New York City unaccompanied by an adult. You couldn't count me as an adult, I was only fifteen.

How, you might ask, would our parents allow us to do this? Our ballet teacher had originally planned on going with us, but with her ever-ready flair for the dramatic she suddenly made the decision to fly and meet us there.

It was the early 1950s, that long-ago era when danger was not always on the edge of our minds.

The first day they arrived in New York their teacher met a man at the Empire State Building and ditched Mom and her friends to have a wild and romantic love affair. Mom's novel revolved around the lively drama of the two weeks she and her young friends lived alone at the YWCA in New York City.

"This is the strangest place," I thought to myself the second day I was there. It was a feeling that was dawning on me, slowly seeping in.

Being in New York City caused my mind to shift. People were alert, listening closely to conversations. Earnest really, and on the other hand, detached.

The city was alive at all hours of the night. People eating spaghetti dinner at 11:30 p.m. in an Italian restaurant right off Broadway after the theater. Young women were dashing into all-night beauty salons to have their hair dyed, coming out completely transformed.

The whole place made my mind drop. I couldn't stop mentally staring. I thought about my parents at home on Layton Avenue in Milwaukee watching the 10:00 p.m. newscast, beginning to nod off in their chairs. Here, people were just getting started.

Life felt like it was opening up to new possibilities, to new potentials.

I didn't want to go to sleep. I wanted to be out in the city seeing all of these extraordinary things.

Mom's sense of wonder that awakened in this early journey continued throughout her life. She passed away before she could complete the book, and she asked if I would write the rest of it if she died before it was done. I agreed.

I began to write her New York City adventure, but our time together at the end of her life kept coming out instead. While facing death together, Mom and I learned how to live. This story is alive in me and worthy of sharing, and the novel set in the '50s will have to wait.

I found this handwritten note in a folder of Mom's and it felt like it was a description of what she discovered at the end of her life.

"This is the real me."

"What do you mean?"

"This, this right now. This is really me. I can feel it. I have been dancing to someone else's tune, but now I am me. This easygoing, smooth, not-so-much-thinking me. I'm not tense. I'm not feeling as if I should be somewhere else, doing something different. I feel like I should be right here, breathing in this moment. It feels perfect."

How she got to this feeling of perfection is a tale worth telling.

While Mom did not complete a book while she was alive, her life was the true novel that she was always seeking. I feel honored to be the one to write it with her.

Mom, this one's for you. Your first completed book. While you are not here with me in this world, I know you are smiling in spirit, and I couldn't have done it without you.

Chapter Two

Love

You are the best daughter that any mom could hope for. You're my daughter and my friend, an unusual combination that I cherish every day. It's always a BLAST to talk to you. I find out things I never knew about and I laugh a lot. We have so much fun—like our drives to and from Seattle. I'll always remember our day among the arches in Moab. What fun! I love you a lot.

My story with Mom and her life and death is ultimately about love.

This was not the fairy-tale version of love, but the rich, full-spectrum kind of love that at times challenged every ounce of us.

Love is our essence and it is a full way of being. Love is not always soft. Love can hurt. Love can heal. Coming from love in everything that one does is no straightforward task, but those who achieve it have a way of changing the world.

Mom lived her life from love at the end. She learned, she grew, and in the midst of her path with cancer she healed. She did not heal her cancer, but she healed her heart and she healed her soul. None of us leave this life alive, but some of us leave this life with health in the depth of our beings.

My journey with Mom as we approached her cancer and her death awakened me to a place of compassion that I am still integrating and figuring out. My relationship with her taught me to face problems with an open heart, even when it felt impossible to do.

Mom was awakened and enlightened in the end, but she was also human and a lot of fun; her vibrant personality radiated in everything she did. Sometimes it's the little things in life that define us even more than the larger choices we make.

Mom adored technology, especially her cell phone. She was technologically challenged, but loved technology and cell phones. The polarity of these two personality traits caused frustration and many ridiculous phone calls to my brother and me over the years.

I remember back when I was a teenager. She and Dad had recently gotten divorced, and Mom was producing the television guide for Wisconsin Public Television. They had gotten a Wang computer that Mom enjoyed calling the "Wang-er Dang-er."

I would go to visit her after school and she would be typing in code on the computer to make it print. If the code wasn't entered exactly right, the computer wouldn't print, and various curse words could be heard from the hallway as I walked in.

This began Mom's love/hate relationship with computers and technology.

Programming the VCR to record shows on television became an epic battle for Mom and conversations filled with frustration and hilarity for my brother and me. Mike was living in Paris after college and his phone rang at three in the morning. He answered the phone sleepily, and it was Mom in a panic calling to find out how to set up the VCR after the power had gone out. He led her through it groggily from four thousand miles away.

Mom loved computers but always fought with them. It was a personal insult to her that they didn't behave for her. Mike fielded most of the phone calls about her computers, and I think he might still have some post-traumatic stress because of it.

When cell phones really started to take off Mom fell in love with them. She treasured her cell phone, and when they evolved to smartphones, Mom became even more hooked.

She played Angry Birds, solitaire, mahjong, and hearts. Occasionally, we would be out to dinner and I would catch her playing a quick game of solitaire because she was bored with the conversations around her.

Her phone was always close. She talked on it for hours, and often it would run out of batteries in the middle of a sentence.

When Mom had her voice box removed because of her cancer and couldn't talk on the phone like she enjoyed, she was devastated. She even lost a bit of interest in it and would often leave it on silent.

Over the course of her cancer treatment, there were many times I didn't know if she was dead or alive because she wasn't answering her phone. I would have to call someone to go check on her, and sure enough, her phone was turned off.

I spent many hours cursing the silent mode.

My brother came up with the brilliant idea of a nanny cam and we hooked one up at her house. Mom knew about it, of course, and loved the idea because I could check on her and make sure she hadn't fallen. More advancements in technology! She was thrilled.

She often expressed how amazing it was to live a lifetime that began with no televisions when she was a kid and that evolved to a world with televisions, computers, cell phones, and then smartphones. Her mind was always open and wondering what the next big thing would be.

There was a fascinating moment in the midst of her dying process. She had been moved to her final rehab place and she was starting to lose touch with this reality. She thought she was back in the 1990s and was sweetly telling me how she loved meeting me for dinner and how much she enjoyed it when she walked up and I was sitting at a restaurant waiting for her. She would anticipate hearing about my adventures and her heart would be full.

In the midst of this recollection, her granddaughter Abby called on FaceTime and she talked with her for a bit.

When she got off of the phone, Mom's eyes were as big as plates and she kept saying, "That was AMAZING, that was AMAZING!" At first I thought she was teasing because Abby had been bouncing off of the walls on FaceTime with her, but then I realized her mind was in 1990 and she just had a video chat with her granddaughter! How astonishing must that have been? It was a thing out of a science fiction novel in the 1990s to talk on the phone and be able to see who you were talking to. Mom's mind was blown and it made her happy.

Another thing that thrilled her was Starbucks. She loved her cappuccinos. It is my belief that Starbucks was founded just to make Mom happy. No offense to all of the other awesome coffee places out there, but Starbucks was the place for her.

I actually don't know what Mom must have done before Starbucks was created.

Every good road trip, short or long, started with a visit to Starbucks where we would get a coffee and a treat.

The funniest thing was that Mom couldn't handle caffeine or dairy. Mom was a walking set of contradictions. It kept those of us who loved her on our toes.

One of my favorite memories of her was when I was in college in the early nineties. Our hometown, Madison, Wisconsin, has an awesome area called State Street where people could walk and shop and eat and drink. Mom and I were spending a day on State Street and I wanted her to try espresso. Coffee shops were not at every corner back then—it was a new phenomenon.

So, Mom and I had a double espresso. You would have thought the two of us were drunk! The espresso hit us with a buzz that had us laughing and stumbling along having the time of our lives. That's when I knew Mom had some trouble with caffeine. Fun trouble, but trouble nonetheless.

After our initial espresso outing, Mom realized she needed to be creative in her coffee order and she discovered decaf soy cappuccinos. She drank them with gusto and enjoyed them with all of her heart.

One day we were going for a drive to the Jemez Mountains near Albuquerque, and the Starbucks we stopped at was closed for some reason. You would have thought the world had come to an end. We managed to enjoy the day without it, but launching a trip, however small, wasn't the same without our Starbucks.

She and I were a great mix of pure heart and a lot of laughter when we got together.

You bring so much love and light and joy and abundance
to so many people that I hope all of it comes right back at you!

And, of course, you light up my life with all your wonderful goofiness, too. I can see you in my mind's eye doing your "morning dance," and I can hear your comments that make me laugh out loud. I love you lots!

Chapter Three

Snap Out of It!

I t was 2012 and life was moving along. Mom and I were both living in Albuquerque in houses across town from each other. She was in her early seventies, exploring life through hiking, tutoring, taking parts as an extra in movies, and hanging out with her friends. There was a part of her that was dissatisfied, and she was trying to figure out what kind of work to do and how to feel fulfilled, but she was entertaining herself regardless.

I was in my early forties, with a vibrant business and social life. I spent my days talking with clients, developing intuition classes, going to dinner, listening to live music, traveling, exploring, and just living. Mom and I got together often, but we also had our own focus and lives.

All of a sudden, the world stopped.

Mom and I were going to a Halloween party. She was dressed up as Katy Perry with a blue wig, short metallic-silver skirt, fitted fishnet pink top, and black platform boots. While she was putting on her makeup she found a lump on her neck.

She had a tumor.

There was an immediate awakening to her mortality. It was as though someone slapped us both and said, "Snap out of it! Your life, this moment, matters. Your time here on this earth is not eternal."

"Wake up!"

Mom's doctors had difficulty identifying whether the tumor was cancer, but they decided to remove her thyroid gland. It was a year later that she had the surgery that changed her life and whole demeanor, but this was our initial foray into her treatment.

I remember her first surgery like it was yesterday. We went early in the morning. Mom could not eat before the surgery, and when I picked her up in my car, she told me she was starving. She looked like she had not slept, and her funky short gray haircut was sticking up in all directions like bird feathers. She walked into the hospital with as much confidence as she could muster, her tall dancer's body striding to the waiting room with style.

With all her bravado Mom was nervous, but when her team came she was happy to see that they were all female doctors. When Mom grew up, she had two choices for professions: nurse or teacher. Throughout her life, Mom had gone to countless marches and gatherings to fight for women's equal rights, and she smiled brightly at the doctors who represented the result of those efforts.

Mom immediately engaged with the surgeon and anesthesiologist, asking questions about her surgery and then talking to them about their lives and who they were. She connected with them as human beings as well as doctors, and they were like a group of friends at a party within a few minutes.

Her medical team all joked around and Mom was laughing, putting a brave face on a scary scenario. They gave her a sedative, and when

Mom was wheeled away to surgery they played, "Somewhere Over the Rainbow," by the Hawaiian artist Iz. Mom was singing loudly along with the song, "Somewhere over the rainbow, way up high. There's a land that I heard of once in a lullaby . . . Someday I'll wish upon a star, wake up where the clouds are far behind me."

The song echoed down the hallway, a cheery contrast to the stark walls of the hospital. This became a theme song for Mom throughout the rest of her life.

The surgery was supposed to take a couple of hours, but it wound up lasting five. I knew something was wrong and I began to get really nervous as the minutes ticked away. By the time the surgeon came out, I was relieved to see her, but I received hard news.

The tumor was definitely cancer and it was not contained. It had spread into the soft tissue of the neck around the thyroid. The surgeon had done her best but was uncertain if she had gotten it all.

Ouch.

I had to go in to see Mom with that news. She had gotten through surgery, which was awesome, but she had a potentially rough road ahead of her. Little did we know how rough it would be.

Mom was high from the anesthesia and smiling brightly when I went to sit with her. She wanted to know how it went and I told her gently that it was cancer. At the time she was too drugged to process the information. She kept telling me she loved me and how happy she was that she had made it through the surgery. I gave up trying to convey the news and just held her hand and told her I loved her.

Over the next couple of days, she learned the extent of the surgery and of the cancer that she had. Mom had a rare thyroid cancer called Hurthle Cell Carcinoma.

The prognosis was pretty optimistic initially. I remember going to a follow-up visit with her surgeon, who was an engaging and stylish woman with high-heeled shoes that Mom coveted. We all sat down for an hour meeting, talking about her type of cancer and the difficulties it could cause.

The doctor said that with Hurthle Cell, Mom could expect more surgeries along the way, but that she could live a long life. We had the impression that the cancer would be a nuisance, but it would be relatively simple to handle.

During the next year, Mom began to struggle with her breathing. We went frequently to the ear, nose, and throat doctor, and he couldn't diagnose that her breathing issue was associated with her cancer. Looking back, it seems like it was obvious, but we did not fully understand how Hurtle Cell worked at the time. Her doctors did not have experience with her type of cancer because it was so rare. None of them had seen it in their practice, so they failed to explain to us how it could potentially spread.

This brings up the imperfections of doctors and of diagnostic tools and of so many aspects of medicine. In retrospect, do I wish there had been better doctors? Do I wish that we had pushed for them to figure things out faster? On some levels, yes, and on some levels, no. Spending our days fighting the system could have been potentially more destructive than the cancer.

I would say that Mom's intuition and knowledge of her own body was strong. She knew she needed more help than she was getting. She kept pushing the doctors for more tests and more answers because she did not feel like she was getting the care she needed, which was true.

In that year, Mom continued to struggle to breathe, and exercise became more and more laborious. A short walk around the block would leave her winded. She was an active person who loved to hike for miles and explore, so this was tremendously upsetting.

At a certain point in that year, life began to be more precious. I began to see Mom's mortality, and an uncertainty about the future rose up in my heart.

During this time, I went with Mom to Seattle to visit Mike, his wife Kim, and their children Chris and Abby. We all traveled to the Olympic Peninsula together. We decided to go for a hike in the forest. There was a beautiful stream running through the dense trees and we were eager to explore. Mom's inability to walk far meant that Abby would have a buddy while the rest of us hiked. I came down the path and discovered them making goofy faces at each other on a park bench, laughing hysterically.

While Mom would have loved to have hiked with us, she found the simple joy of being silly with her granddaughter to be equal or even better. Her body made her stop, and in stopping she had a meaningful interaction.

As a family, we had a glimpse into the future of loss for Mom. She began to lose freedom.

Instead of dwelling on the loss, she stopped and found the places she could enjoy. Her ability to transform hardship into something beautiful began to awaken.

Chapter Four

An Impossible Choice

Upon returning to Albuquerque, we went to more doctors and specialists, and no one could give Mom a diagnosis. She was a strong advocate for her own health and was determined to find an answer, so she got permission from her insurance to go to MD Anderson, an acclaimed cancer center in Houston, to get thorough testing.

Mom's perseverance served her. Her new team of doctors in Houston found that her thyroid cancer had spread in her neck.

They were going to need to do one of two surgeries. One would remove her voice box and the other would remove her swallowing tube. She was either forever going to have to breathe through her neck and talk with the aid of a talking device or forever get nourishment from an external feeding tube in her stomach.

The two experiences that Mom loved in life more than anything, eating and talking, were on the line.

There are people who eat because they have to. Not Mom. She was always thinking about food. She would tell me dreams she would have about certain foods and menus. If she went on a vacation, one of the most important things about the trip for her were the restaurants she got to go to and the food she got to try. Mediterranean chicken, Pho, Pad Thai, elaborate pastas, tiramisu, and key lime pie were some of her favorites. Most conversations with Mom included what she had eaten that day, and the next meal was always on her mind.

Mom was also a constant conversationalist. She was not someone who monologued; she wanted to hear your opinion as well, but she didn't love silence. Her curiosity was way too active for that.

When we took road trips, we talked the whole way, whether it was a two-hour jaunt or a twenty-hour trek. When we weren't together, we talked for hours on the phone.

She loved to pick apart movies, talk about relationships and analyze people, tell stories about her life, and think out loud about politics and history. She asked me questions and engaged in what I was going through and would dive into any subject I wanted to investigate. Talking about life and death and everywhere in between was fascinating for her. To take away the ability to talk seemed like it was taking away the piece of her that was at her essence. Her voice was a big part of all of my memories of Mom before the surgery.

I think about Mom receiving the information that her only two options to live required her to make an impossible decision.

I think about where in the world I was and why I wasn't there with her when she went to MD Anderson for the first time. I remember her stories about taking shuttles and taxis from her Motel 6 to get all of her tests done, and I remember the stunned phone call she made to me when she got the news about the surgeries.

She was alone and having to deal with some of the biggest news of her life. The importance of being there became obvious after she had her next surgery. There was no way someone could adjust to so many new ways of being without some form of help. But, before that happened, Mom was always an independent person who made her own decisions. Did she ask for me to come with her? Did I tell her no? There's no telling, I don't remember.

There's a deep ingrained feeling in our hearts that our parents can take care of themselves. That they are invincible. Many people told me that Mom should have stayed invincible in my eyes—that she never should have let me take care of her to the degree that she did. They were concerned that her needs took me drastically away from my life. It always felt strange when people told me that because it never occurred to me *not* to help her. She was a big part of my life, so taking care of her was a natural progression of our relationship.

Being a part of Mom's path with cancer allowed me to see her in depth, and in love, and in humor. Waking up to the reality that she was *not* invincible and getting to be there for her when she was weak and scared was such a privilege. Her willingness to share this part of her life with me was brave, and together we learned to embrace life fully when faced with death.

Chapter Five

The Comedy and the Tragedy

S ince Mom and I always celebrated life in the midst of a challenge, we planned a trip to Puerto Rico a couple of weeks before her second surgery. The culture there is rich and it's a beautiful island that's alive with color, smells, sounds, and vibrant people. It is a place that restored and strengthened our hearts so we could prepare for what was to come.

On our first day, we climbed around Castillo San Felipe del Morro, a historic castle in Old San Juan. The building was fun to explore, but Mom was really struggling to breathe. Anytime we walked too fast or had to take an incline, she would sound like she was having an asthma attack and we would have to stop so she could catch her breath. This was new for her and new for us, so we realized that we needed to rent a car in order to see the sights.

We drove across the countryside and explored the island while driving. There was profound beauty, and we stopped many times to take in the landscapes and ocean views. One late afternoon while we were on our way home we saw some giant rocks in the ocean being pummeled by huge waves. The waves crashed onto the rocks and the water was flung into the sky like confetti. We wound our way through the narrow streets of the small town to see this close-up.

When we got near, the park next to the ocean was alive with a street fair, and people were on donkeys and in carts, partying and dancing. We found parking and walked out to the waves and watched for at least an hour as the water danced in front of us, crashing into the rocks and falling in dazzling patterns and shapes. The music was all around us and people were laughing and playing in the ocean.

"So beautiful. The beauty, the celebration, and the chaos," Mom said.

"So beautiful," I replied.

When we returned home that night we were starving so we went to dinner at a Chinese restaurant in our hotel. It was near to closing and we were grateful they let us order.

Unfortunately, we were served fried rice that had a foul flavor of dirty socks. We felt badly but we sent it back. We were not ones to send food back lightly, but this was inedible.

All of a sudden, we heard crashing and commotion, and I saw one of the cooks pull out a knife that looked like a machete, and the other cook had to hold him back from coming out to the dining room. They were screaming at each other in another language.

The one cook was clearly hell-bent on coming out and killing us for returning our food.

Mom and I couldn't help it and we broke out laughing and had to leave quickly so we didn't make them angrier. Laughing at the most inappropriate circumstances seemed to be a forté for us.

As we returned giggling to our room, Mom sat on the bed and started sobbing.

"I don't want to die," she said. "I don't want to leave all this beauty and this fun." She was inconsolable.

I sat with her and let her cry. She started losing her ability to breathe, and she said, "I can't even cry anymore because I can't breathe. I need to breathe, I need to feel, I need to live."

"I'm so sorry, Mom," was all I could say, and I put my arm around her while she sobbed and struggled for breath. There were no words that could help at that moment. Just love.

As she got through it and processed her emotions out loud, we made a commitment that in the midst of the hardship that was to come, we would remember to look at beautiful things and have whatever adventures we could have.

The next day, I asked her what she would like to do before we left. She told me she was afraid of getting into the ocean because she was having trouble breathing, but she would like to get out in the waves with me and float. She knew that after her surgery it was possible she would never be able swim again, and she wanted to be in the ocean one last time.

I took her hand and we went out into the waves. They were gentle that day. We brought out a boogie board, and she bobbed around on it and floated and soaked in the experience of the ocean.

I kept looking over at her and saw how peaceful she became knowing I was there for her if she needed me, but also just enjoying the feeling of being one with the vast and powerful ocean.

She had a gentle smile on her face as she got out, and she thanked me for helping her with her fears. We sat under a palm tree on the soft sand and watched the wind blow the leaves in abstract patterns, and we bathed in the sweetness of just being there together. It was the calm before the storm.

That night she ordered her favorite drink, a vodka gimlet, and had a gigantic shrimp meal. I admired how she always ordered whatever she wanted regardless of the calories or cost and how she ate her food with gusto.

We celebrated her life. We celebrated our lives together. We celebrated life itself.

And then we walked into the storm.

Chapter Six

The In-Between

When I found out I was going to be a grandma, it put a big smile on my face.

Having children has been one of the most awesome experiences and has truly enriched my life. I have loved seeing my children grow from a tiny infant to a toddler to a teenager and to an adult. I often would sit back in amazement and curiosity to see how each of my children would be. It's been fascinating.

And now, I get to see my grandchildren grow! They are creative, smart, talkative, happy, and curious and life has only just begun for them. We have so much fun together.

When I think of Christopher and Abby, it brings tears of joy to my eyes. All of the generations before them live in their hearts.

When we got home from Puerto Rico, Mike, his wife Kim, Chris, and Abby came to see Mom before her surgery.

We did all of our favorite things together: the zoo, Santa Fe, great restaurants, ghost towns, and hiking. Mom was thrilled to spoil her grandkids with hugs, special activities, and candy. Lots of candy.

Life was always spectacular when we all got together, but there was an extra weight to this moment. We knew that whatever surgery Mom chose would change our relationship with her to some degree.

I think about the kids: Chris was seven and Abby was four. Processing big stuff like life, death, cancer, and losing voices was hard enough for us adults. For someone whose brain was still figuring life out, it must have been mind-boggling. We all did the best we could with navigating the big stuff while also having a good time, and Mike and Kim did a great job supporting them through it and so did Mom.

She wanted a special day with Chris and Abby before they left. Taking them to the dollar store and letting them pick out as many things as they wanted was one of Mom's favorite things to do. When Mike, Kim, and I went to pick them up after their day together, all three of them were adorned with Hawaiian leis and funny straw cowboy hats. They were golfing around Mom's house with plastic golf clubs, and they had drawn pictures all over their arms and legs with face paint. The kids were on a sugar high and didn't sleep for hours, but they were filled with happiness because of their grandma. They traveled home to Seattle with big smiles on their faces.

Mike stayed and had some extra time with Mom and then flew with her to Houston to do the final preparations for surgery.

Along with the doctors, Mike helped Mom choose the procedure that would take her voice box. When she got it she would never be able to talk normally again.

Once they made their decision, they realized they had two days before the surgery and they didn't want to just sit around. They threw around some wild ideas on what to do with their time and even pondered going to New Orleans, but realized it was too far to go to really enjoy it.

They settled on Kemah Boardwalk on Galveston Bay, which is a place like Coney Island with rides, games, and fun food. As they walked around, they saw a giant speedboat with teeth painted on the front of it to make it look like a shark. Since Mom wouldn't be able to get in the water again after surgery, she said, "Let's do that!" Mike said, "Awesome!" They sped around the Bay with wild abandon and laughed as they were thrown side to side. Luckily they had brought their luggage in the car because they emerged from the experience completely drenched from head to toe.

Aunt Betty and Kim joined them back in Houston, and they all went out early the night before surgery so Mom could have a last meal before her life was changed forever. The dinner of choice was at a fancy Italian restaurant, and they overindulged in pasta and tiramisu, talking and sharing memories.

I had given them a voice recorder so we could document the sound of Mom's voice before she lost it.

When I listened to the recording, there was a lot of laughter and many stories. I could sense a little edge of nerves in Mom's voice while she was talking. She had a strong and intelligent way of speaking and an enthusiastic tone to everything she expressed. Her voice was loud, clear, and lively. The subjects up for discussion were wildly varied, her humor swung from the irreverent to the absurd, and she jumped around from laughter to deep thoughts.

Their voices became subdued when they paid their bill and headed back to the hotel. The unknown future loomed ahead.

The next day, Mom went into surgery. It turned out Mom never had to make the choice of which procedure to have; the cancer chose for her. It had spread too close to her voice box and she had it removed and also had a tracheostomy, or a breathing hole, opened in her neck so that she was never able to swim or be in the water again.

They also had to remove part of her esophagus and build a swallowing tube from the skin of her right leg. This was an innovative and intricate procedure that had not existed two years before, and the whole process took about nine hours under anesthesia.

Mike and Aunt Betty were there for the surgery and initial recovery, and I was going later for the second shift to help her get out of the hospital and come home to Albuquerque.

Chapter Seven

Waking Up from Surgery

I try to open my eyes several times and everything is a blur. My eyes just won't open. Finally, I squint and see that I'm lying in a bed in a small, dark space and I feel as if I can't move. I feel as if I have a noose around my neck and I can't breathe. Thoughts begin to come to me slowly at first. Where am I? What's happening? Where is everyone? Why am I alone? Have I been buried alive?

I feel as if I'm in a dark, small hole and no one is here to help me.

I start to see some objects above me and wonder if I am in a closet? Am I in a deep, dark closet where no one will ever find me? Has someone closed the door, maybe locked the door and I can't get out? I feel trapped and scared.

And then the worst thing that can happen, happens. I try to scream and no sound comes from my mouth. That's when an immense panic fills my very being.

I can't speak. Is someone strangling me? Will I never be found?

I struggle to move and can't. My arms, my legs, my knees, nothing will move.

And then a memory slowly comes to the forefront of my mind. Oh, I've had surgery. I can't speak because my voice box is gone.

But, where is everybody? Where are my son and daughter-in-law and sister? Why aren't they here with me? Why am I not in the ICU as planned? I should have monitors checking my vitals. Has something gone horribly wrong? Am I dying? Have they dumped me in the morgue, but I'm not really dead? I need help.

My hazy vision slowly detects a small, long light in the room and a blurry image of someone moving into the room pulling a large cart.

I finally manage to sit up.

A small, older woman approaches my bed and I try to grab ahold of her. I finally have enough sense to pantomime writing something and God came to me as she handed me just what I needed: a piece of paper and a pen.

She has a thick accent from an Eastern European or maybe Middle Eastern country. She can barely read my words.

"I'm starving, is someone starving me?"

"I'm being held against my will."

"Where are my things? My cell phone, my purse? Have they been taken from me?"

No one cares. No one loves me. No one is coming to save me.

A memory flashes across my mind, coming to me unbidden. I'm sitting in a chair at the edge of our living room in Greendale, Wisconsin. My mom is hovering over me keeping me pinned to the chair. She is angry at me for something I wouldn't do and she keeps me pinned down until my dad comes home to save me.

I come back to this dark room and I am writing frantically to this woman with the cart. Words are written every which way, coming out fast and furious as my scattered mind filled with anesthesia thinks about needing this and needing that.

I finally realize that I need to have her call someone. "Call my son," I write down in one corner of the paper. I realize though that I don't know his cell number. I never needed to memorize it because I just push auto dial.

"Call my daughter," I write. I know her number because I live in the same city as her and often have to give out her number. I scribble down her number and I write it so fast that it's not legible. I write it again and get it wrong because I am in such a hurry. Finally, I get the number correctly and write down to call her because I need help.

And my poor daughter Liz gets a call in the middle of the night far away in Albuquerque, New Mexico, from a woman she doesn't know who's speaking in broken English and shouting, "Emergency, emergency, a woman needs your help!" Liz knows I have had surgery and has panicked thoughts that I might be dying.

When I received that call, I was initially terrified and confused. Wasn't Mom in the hospital?

Once I figured out what was going on, I had the woman put the phone on speaker so I could explain to Mom where she was and calm her down as best as I could. She couldn't respond to me so I had to have the woman translate what Mom was writing. This was Mom and my first encounter with the fact that she had completely lost her voice, and it was a shocker. It took a long time for both of us to settle down from the intensity of the moment.

I called my brother and he went and sat with her.

Mom said she never saw the woman who helped her again, and she was convinced she was an angel who came to save her from her living nightmare.

When I think about not being able to talk, I can feel it viscerally and it is intense. Not being able to scream if I needed to scream and not being able to make a sound would make me feel terror. Our voice is a part of our survival mechanism.

Beyond survival, our voice contains so much of our personality. I can't imagine Mom having to face never being able to talk freely and fluidly again, not being able to laugh with any sound to it, not being able to make herself heard in social situations, not being able to make a phone call, and not being able to tell stories.

Her life was forever changed in an instant by this surgery. And so was mine.

During the year between Mom's two surgeries, she was like a caterpillar weaving a chrysalis. Her chrysalis was internal and was constructed from love, adaptability, fortitude, and determination. Some part of her knew she had to transform in a powerful way in order to transcend her diagnosis and live an illuminated life. When she went under anesthesia this second time, she was reborn. Her body was rearranged during surgery, but her whole being went through a metamorphosis as well. Layers of her personality were shed and she emerged a vibrant butterfly, but one with a broken wing who needed help sharing her beauty with the world. This moment of emerging showed the equal fragility and strength of her new self.

I had the honor to be her caregiver, but I walked in unaware of the intensity of the supporting role I was about to take on.

Chapter Eight

The Strength to Survive

A week after her surgery at MD Anderson, I went to see Mom, get her out of the hospital, and bring her home to Albuquerque. As much as I had wanted to go to Houston for her surgery, someone needed to be with her when she was released from medical care.

There was nothing that prepared me for what I was about to experience.

My friend Jan and I flew to Houston. We were supposed to arrive in time to meet Aunt Betty and the nurses so they could train me on how to take care of Mom before they released her that day. Our connecting flight from Dallas got canceled, and the only way we could get to Houston in time for her discharge was to rent a car and drive.

We got to MD Anderson close to midnight. By the time we arrived, there was very little staff; my aunt had flown home and we were presented with a scary sight.

Mom looked like Frankenstein. Her neck was as fat as her head, with stitches that made it look like someone had chopped off her head and sewn it back on again. Since they had made a swallowing tube out of the skin on her right leg, there was a long gash from her knee to her groin with stitches all up her thigh and tubes hanging out of the wound to drain the infection.

She had a feeding tube hanging out of her nose that was her only way of eating, and an orderly handed me poorly written paperwork on how to use it.

She was breathing out of a hole in her neck from the tracheostomy. This needed suctioning or she could choke and die. Someone gave me a two-minute crash course on suctioning, which requires you to stick a tube down the hole she was breathing out of in her neck and suction out snot that could harden and block her airway. She also had to have a larytube, a plastic tube about three-quarters of an inch long, inserted in the tracheostomy so it would not close up.

Mom was a walking time bomb, or multiple time bombs, that even a trained nurse might be afraid to take out of the hospital. An orderly casually wheeled her into a hotel room next to the hospital, dumped a bunch of bags of stuff that were in a total disarray on the bed, and left us.

In my mind, there was no reason to have let her out of the hospital with me that night, but Mom had already signed the release papers. She was clearly drugged on oxycodone and felt invincible—but I was in shock.

I understand that anyone who looked at Mom would want to give her pain medication, but she had become overdependent on oxycodone in the week she was in the hospital after her surgery. Yes, she needed it for pain, but she was taking it to an extreme and it made her completely unable to function.

She was invincible in her mind. She seemed unfazed by the fact that she was breathing out of a hole in her neck and that she could choke and die. She was smiling and laughing and happy to be out of the hospital, and she was making noises with her talking stick. The next second she would seem checked out, dazed, and unable to think clearly.

Mom was drunk and happy to be out of the hospital, and Jan and I were terrified. Mom sat on the bed and immediately fell sound asleep, and we looked at each other in horror.

We took turns being up with her that first night. While it was my turn, I fell asleep for a second. I woke up with a start at the sound of Mom starting to choke. This was my first terrifying suctioning experience. As she struggled to breathe, I yelled for Jan and we fought to figure out what we were supposed to do to save her. Just the stress of looking down a gaping hole into Mom's chest was enough, but I had to turn on a loud suction machine that pulled in air, stick a tube into her breathing hole, and pull out a mucous plug that was blocking her airway.

We did it and the stress of it made me sit up ramrod straight; I was awake for the rest of the night so I wouldn't be caught unaware again and miss Mom needing me.

It was one of the worst nights of my life.

I had no time to adjust to or integrate in my mind and heart how injured and debilitated Mom looked. She was forever changed and suddenly I was responsible for her life, her safety, and her ability to breathe.

I learned as she lived with her tracheostomy that very few people knew how to suction. Every time we went to a hospital as her disease progressed, we would have to find a respiratory therapist to train the staff. Yet I was left to train *myself* on the first night I was with Mom.

The next morning, Jan and I started going through the five bags of stuff to try to figure out what was in them.

There was feeding tube food, which was a mixture of high fructose corn syrup and vitamins. Mom had a voracious appetite, and *this* was her food for the next month while her swallowing tube that they had constructed from the skin of her leg healed. We were saddened by the quality of food available for those who have to eat this way.

Jan was the only one who could figure out how to do the feeding tube without the "food" spilling out all over the floor. We had no training except for a piece of paper with crappy instructions.

Next we found her medicine. It was in a total disarray; we had no idea when she was supposed to have her pills. But somehow, even though Mom was totally drugged on oxy, she knew when she took her medication. She had a bad heart along with all of her other ailments and was prone to atrial fibrillation and high blood pressure, so we had to make sure we didn't miss her heart medication.

The surgery caused her to lose her sense of taste. I think it had something to do with closing off her airway through her mouth. This was lucky because she had to take her pills crushed up in water since she couldn't swallow anything other than liquids.

She breathed completely through the opening in her throat. She regained a little bit of her sense of smell and taste along the way, but it would have to be a strong smell or a strong taste.

The next thing we had to deal with was her larytube, the plastic tube that was inserted into her tracheostomy and kept it from closing up. The hole in her neck that she would breathe through for the rest of her life could get infected if it wasn't treated properly. This is what we gathered from another piece of paper with instructions on it. She had to learn to remove the larytube, clean the mucous out of it, and then insert it back into her neck. It scared her to do this, and it took over a month for her to attempt it, so I got the honor of doing it, initially. It was always covered in snot and it always choked her to take it in and out of her neck. It was awful, but I guess since she had wiped my snot and my butt the first years of my life, this was the least I could do.

The tracheostomy created more phlegm because Mom didn't get the natural moisturization that came with breathing through her nose or throat. The opening went straight to her lungs and the dry air caused mucous. She would need to cough the phlegm up quickly so it didn't block her airway. When she coughed it up, it wasn't coughed into her mouth, it came straight out of the opening. She had to catch it in her hand with a tissue, if she was lucky enough to have one ready.

Mom hacked up phlegm for the rest of her life—pretty often, pretty grossly, and pretty publicly. This was a bit socially challenging at times. However! She learned to live breathing through a hole in her neck and always having the possibility of choking on her snot. That's pretty amazing.

Mom's leg wound was the least of our worries, but it was still a wonder. It was cut from her knee to her thigh, sewn back together, and was draining through a tube. We had to change the drainage a couple of times a day. Crazy how that was the least grotesque.

The biggest problem we encountered was Mom's overreliance on oxy. They sent us home with four giant bottles of liquid oxycodone. Luckily, Mom and I were able to talk about everything, and she was not opposed to talking with me about how much she was taking. She said that while she was in the hospital, if she asked for pain medication, she got it. They didn't attempt to wean her off of it or question how much pain she was in when she asked for it.

Looking at Mom's situation, I could understand her desire to not only dull her physical pain, but also to escape the reality of not being able to talk, breathing through a hole in her neck, eating through a feeding tube, and dealing with a scary cancer.

She would get extremely agitated and angry when she didn't get her oxy, and then become complacent and not be able to function once she had it. Mom was like a wild animal needing to eat when she wanted her drug. And she wanted it often. And she wanted it for something other than her physical pain.

I sat her down and said, "I totally understand wanting to numb out right now, but if you want to not only stay alive, but actually live, we have to wean you off of this medicine so that you're just taking it for pain, not for numbing."

Mom had really wanted to live after this surgery and she was afraid she might not. Losing her to this medication would have been a terrible thing. Then, there would have been no point in her surviving. We would have lost her spirit.

We talked about this and she agreed. She hadn't wanted to numb out; they had just given her the medication and she figured they knew what they were doing by giving it to her as often as they did. The prescription read "as needed," and it was a *massive* dose.

We made a plan for her to take the oxy further and further apart until she was only taking it for pain. She alternated it with Tylenol, and she was able to stay more alert while still taking care of the discomfort from her injuries.

Finally, on the second day out of the hospital after another scary night with suctioning, there was a knock on the door from a home healthcare attendant. He taught us suctioning and how to care for Mom's tracheotomy. He also helped sort through the pills and instructed us more thoroughly about how to deal with the feeding tube. Knowing how to do everything definitely helped, but it did not take away the difficulty of facing life and death consistently with Mom.

That week we had appointments with doctors and learned more about Mom's long-term care. Slowly Mom got a little better, and slowly Jan and I became more adept at tending to her needs.

We were overwhelmed and astounded that there wasn't a better system of discharging a patient with as many issues as Mom had.

The next big question was how to get Mom home safely. She was still so fragile, and yet we couldn't stay in Houston forever. It had only been two weeks since her surgery. Jan's husband Tony offered to rent an RV and drive her across Texas to Albuquerque, but we were worried that kind of trip would be too hard on Mom.

Flying seemed scary because she might need to be suctioned mid-flight, and we were concerned about the lack of room to suction her and the distress that it could cause us and potentially the other passengers.

There were no good choices, but we had to pick one. We decided on flying, and we wheeled her through the airport with all of the tubes and bags hanging off of her.

I said a lot of prayers before and during the flight, but we made it to Albuquerque safe and sound, and I brought Mom home with me to continue on her road to recovery. She stayed at my house a few months as she learned slowly how to look after herself.

Over the course of those months, she got used to her larytube, even though it scared her. She was able to swallow again, so the feeding tube was taken out. This was an incredibly happy development for Mom. She could finally eat solid food again!

We slowly got her off of oxy, and she began to learn how to deal with the emotional aspects of her new life. This was an arduous task for her because she couldn't process out loud like most of us do. No one could understand her. I was learning to, but it was not an easy task.

Mom had to go within and find all the strength that she had to survive.

Chapter Nine

I Am Your Mother

I cannot talk normally although I have been very creative in finding ways to communicate. I have what I call a "talking stick," which makes me sound like a robot (although my grandson Christopher says I sound like one of the clones from Star Wars). I stick a small tube onto my tongue and I can speak, even though I sound robotic. It's been a lifesaver because I adore talking.

Of course, I do a lot of writing to say what I want to say. I go out and about, and I just write in my many notepads to clerks in stores. It's been interesting to see people's reactions. Most people are fine, but some adults kind of stare at me. Some are understanding and they say something like, "The very best of luck to you."

Children are just wonderful. They want to know how it works and are very curious about it. One day, a friend of Christopher's came over after school and asked a lot of questions about it. Then he said, "It's very interesting to hear about your robot voice, but I am sure sorry you have cancer." What a sweetheart at only eight years old.

I have to admit, not being able to talk gets very frustrating since what I say is usually very abbreviated and I'm a talker and love to tell stories.

I want to take a weighted pause in order to delve deeper into Mom's massive loss—the loss of her voice. The physical traumas Mom went through were nothing compared to the emotional trauma of losing her ability to talk.

So I'll rewind for a minute to immediately after her surgery at MD Anderson. While she was still in the hospital, Mom got her electrolarynx. I called this her "talker" or her "talking stick." It was a three-inch-long metal tube that fit in her hand. On the tube there were two buttons, one for a man's voice that was a low buzzing noise and one for a woman's voice that was a higher buzz. It had a straw that stuck out of the top of it that Mom put in her mouth, and the movement of her mouth and tongue made it sound, in theory, like words.

When she got her talker she was so excited to call me and be able to have a conversation. All I could hear was beeping. I couldn't hear the individual words; she just sounded like a robot speaking Morse Code.

It was devastating to Mom that I couldn't understand her. Her heart broke thinking that she might never be able to talk on the phone again. Patience is a dirty word for most of us, and so I just told her that we would work on it and figure out how to communicate.

My heart felt heavy and I feared I might never be able to understand Mom again, but I knew that we would do the best we could to solve the problem.

Mom's electrolarynx made it impossible to hear emotion in her words, and most people could either not decipher what she said at all, or they would just get the basics like yes or no. This was beyond difficult in many places in Mom's journey because people could not understand what she was going through.

Slowly, Mom got better with her talker, and those of us who were close to her became more capable of understanding her. After a couple of months, Mike and I were able to talk on the phone with her and comprehend what she was saying, with the occasional need to have her repeat certain words. Aunt Betty could Skype with her, and the combination of lipreading and her talker worked for them. This was an incredible relief for all of us.

Some of her friends became adept at understanding her as well, but it took a lot of presence to get accustomed to her accent. I called it her accent because learning to understand her was similar to developing the ability to grasp the words of someone who pronounced language differently.

Mom couldn't get counseling because the counselors could not make out her words and did not have the time to figure it out. A family member or friend who knew her needed to be there as an interpreter. As her illness progressed and she became less and less mobile, someone needed to be there with her for almost everything. Often, that person was me, and this was a very intense thing because she had to reveal things to me that she might not normally.

It was very lucky that Mom was not shy, and it was also lucky that she and I were close.

When Mom and I went out together, I introduced her as my "high-tech mom." I found that if people had a positive introduction to her, they would be much more open to talk with her. A lot of people were fascinated that she could speak with her "talking stick," some acted uncomfortable, and most were polite.

Every time we went to a restaurant and Mom began talking, the whole restaurant would turn around and look. Once they saw Mom and her talker they were able to go on eating, but her voice always brought attention and aroused curiousity. Sometimes it made me feel uncomfortable because the whole room became silent for a moment, and it felt like we were in a spotlight. Mom ignored the response and dug into her food with gusto, no matter what.

Occasionally, we would encounter people who were mean. She and I were at a restaurant once and two ladies kept looking at us and scowling. They finally decided to move, but they kept glaring at us and exclaiming loudly how rude we were.

Mom lived at an independent living facility at the end of her life, and a man who lived there would yell at her and tell her to shut up. He didn't understand that she was talking and thought she was just making noise to be annoying.

Being around individuals with cognitive issues and also being around a lot of people with hearing issues could be tough for anyone, but it was especially challenging for Mom with her talking stick. She wound up having to write her conversations down. I have many pocket-sized colorful pads of paper filled with one-sided chats.

"Do you know how to turn on the volume on my cell?"
"Last time I played scrabble I had 2 x's."
"I lose my mind."
"They had a pianist at dinner."
"Is he ok?"
"The water is terrible."
"How far can she go?"

And so on.

On occasion, the people at the facility she lived in wrote her back. A woman wrote, "I like writing to you. Do you always wear a hat?" "I have tumors on my head," Mom responded.

"How long?" she wrote.

"Two years."

The dialogue went on for a while, and I could tell that Mom and the woman were chatting a bit out loud in between what they wrote. I love that someone felt compelled to write to her even though I would guess that the woman could speak.

What I noticed most about Mom's conversations was that they were short sentences. She could communicate through writing and pantomiming and talking a bit, but there was very little depth. It must have been so difficult to have to get to know people without being able to discuss her life, her hobbies, her history, and her dreams.

The loss of her voice required Mom to shift gears. She had always been the life of the party and instead she had to sit back, observe, and listen.

When I could no longer speak, I missed it terribly, but I also heard so many interesting stories. Today, I went to the hospital for an echocardiogram and the woman who took me in to the appointment told me her name was Hope. I wrote her a note asking how she got such a beautiful name.

She said she was born during World War II and they didn't have a lot of money, and her dad left before she was born. "It was a sad time," she said, "and I suppose my mom saw me as a sign of hope. Isn't it funny? I never asked my mom about this. She was such a private person."

I wrote to ask her if she got a new dad and she said no, but her grandpop was her dad. She said, "My mom died when I was 58 years old and every holiday I feel sad because she's not with me."

I have so many times when I hear stories like this that I might not have heard if I could talk. In fact, when I told Hope by mouthing the words that I couldn't talk, she said, "Well then I guess I'll have to do all the talking," and she certainly did.

Mom's personality saved her at this time of her life. She was willing to push through potential awkwardness and strike up a conversation in any way she could. Her natural curiosity and interest in people helped others get over their discomfort and connect with her.

She dyed her hair bright pink and she went out into the world with gusto. She spoke to everyone she could. Children were especially fascinated by her talking stick; she would pretend she was Darth Vader, and they would laugh and laugh together.

She liked to say the quote from *Star Wars*, "I am your father."

One time I couldn't find where she went in a store and then I heard her talker. When I got to her she was surrounded by about ten kids and their parents, and they were all laughing hysterically because Mom was playing the *Jaws* theme on her talker.

Mom could have been scary to people with her talker, her walker, her trach, and her tumors, but most people looked to her spirit and her smile, and the rest wound up not mattering to them.

Chapter Ten

The Sleeping Monster Awakens

Having cancer definitely changed me. I am learning to meditate and I do that several times a day. This has helped me immensely and offered me a sense of peace. My daughter Liz, who is an intuitive healer, has made me some videos with excellent mantras which have helped me stay more positive. My son Mike sent me an article about the benefits of exercise so I'm still walking an hour a day and have kept up my yoga routine. And, in the midst of all that has been going on, I am more aware of the beauty in each day and I feel joy and gratitude for my life.

M om and I were settling into a new life after her surgery. She was trying to find a rhythm with her tracheostomy, her talker, and a new way of eating and swallowing, and she was living an entirely different life that was silent. For about three months after we got home to Albuquerque, she stayed with me. I began to learn how to support her and balance the caregiving with my business and with my life.

We approached it the only way we knew how: with a sense of humor and a willingness to cry and be frustrated at times.

As a daughter, it was heart-wrenching to realize that my role with my mother had forever changed and that she would need my help for the rest of her life. This drastic change in roles was not something I could linger on because there was a constant evolution of problems to solve, but I want to note it and honor it because many people grapple with this at some point in their lives.

During the five years of cancer treatment, there were stages of intense care and then stages where Mom was more independent. At this stage, after surgery, Mom needed constant care. If I left the house, I had to make sure someone was with her. She was not able to call for help. Her tracheostomy was still healing and she had the possibility of choking. Mom was such an independent person that this was very different for her. I am also an independent person and it was different for me. We did the best we could.

My dad's sister, my aunt Linda, is a nurse and came and helped for a while. Various different friends would hang out with Mom while I did errands. Inevitably, I would come home and find Mom and whoever she was with laughing. "Beep beep beep," was Mom's form of laugh and it always made me smile when I heard it. A different kind of infectious laugh than we are used to, but it worked nonetheless.

We fell into a rhythm with each other, and we were lulled into a feeling that everything was okay and we could settle into this way of life. In the midst of this time something devastating happened.

I remember the exact moment I knew Mom was going to die of cancer. We had been informed that the surgery at MD Anderson had gotten all the cancer, and we had believed she would be safe for a while. We knew she would need more treatment eventually, but we thought we had some time.

On a morning in September, three months after her surgery while Mom was staying with me, I hugged her and all illusions were shattered. She had a fist-sized lump that had popped up overnight on her shoulder.

The night before, I had barely slept. I was plagued by a black energy that kept washing over me, making it impossible for me to breathe. I would wake up struggling and feeling terrified. I have always seen the energy of cancer as black and dense, so this dream that haunted me seemed so fitting.

For the whole day after I found the lump, I could not stop crying. I felt a certainty that Mom was going to die from her cancer. *When* of course was not definite, but how and why had shown its ugly head. On that day I fully surrendered to the pain of knowing my mom was dying. There was no option other than to give in to the emotion and to my broken heart. I left the house and cried and cried.

Many times after that day, she and I talked about death and cried together, but in this moment I needed the space to grieve completely without worrying about how it affected her.

I realize now that Mom already knew it was close to her time. I feel like she knew the minute she found her tumor on Halloween almost two years before. She had always seemed certain she was dying, even before we knew it was cancer.

Mom was very intuitive and knew her truth clearly. She was determined from the start to fight the cancer, but some deep part of her comprehended that it was the beginning of the end of her life.

After finding the lump on her shoulder, Mom went back to MD Anderson and was told she had cancer throughout her body. My sister-in law Kim's mom Jackie had flown out to be with her, and they talked with Mom's team to figure out what to do with this new development. There was no set treatment for the metastatic cancer that she had because it was so rare, so they were going to have to try experimental treatments to see if they could slow down the progression of the disease.

This began a new level of intensity to the profoundly challenging and enlightening journey we were on.

When Mom and I contemplated death together, we decided to look at how we could *live* more. She and I made an even more conscious commitment to have as much fun as we could. We agreed to talk about dying when we needed to, but we also agreed to not lose focus on our beautiful life by only thinking about what was coming. We would stay present with what we had in front of us. If she was not well, we would deal with it as best we could. If she was well, we would do what we could to enjoy life.

During this time, Mom wrote a poem.

It's all possible, it's all possible, carpe diem!
I can fly to the moon and see the world from above.
I will marry a pilot and fly to Paree.
I'll capture a pearl in the depths of the sea.
I'll ride horses in Montana, crest the waves at the beach,
Find starfish in the ocean,
Nothing's out of my reach.

It's delightful, delirious, delicious, divine.
It's comical, curious, carnivorous, and fine,
I'll dash and I'll prance.
I'll wish and take a chance.
I'll wiggle and giggle,
And have the last dance.

Chapter Eleven

The Time I Died…Twice

I'm afraid of dying. All of a sudden when I was lying down, I was feeling weird and I realized that I was very afraid. Terrified. Just terrified.

What do I do about the fear of death? How can I go about coming to terms with it?

I believe that we go to spirit and that our spirit lives on. I think that what bothers me is that I will miss being the person that I am in this lifetime. When we die, this being that we are will never exist again and the world of people that I live in will not exist again. Mike will not be Mike. Liz will not be Liz. Betty will not be Betty.

Death is a concept that is difficult to understand. I cling to this world. I want it to exist forever. How can I feel glorious about going to spirit? How do I manage to let go of this life that I am living in now and that I so dearly love?

We were in for an intense ride with Mom's cancer, and she was having to face her mortality, so we pondered what we knew about death.

When approaching the thought of dying, Mom and I had a unique perspective because it was something we encountered quite a bit in our lives together.

I have had two near-death experiences, and Mom and I had talked extensively about them.

The first time I met death, I was in my early twenties and had just moved to the mountains of New Mexico from Wisconsin. In Wisconsin, I loved walking in the rain. I was not accustomed to New Mexico. When it rains here, there is usually lightning involved.

I was walking in the National Forest behind my house with my roommate and our dogs. It was a beautiful day, and then the clouds started rolling in. Before we had a chance to blink, we were caught in a thunderstorm. We were the tallest objects around because the trees were shrub-like junipers.

Lightning was striking all around us and we were running down the mountain trying to get home. Our hair was standing on end, and my dog looked like he had stuck his paw in a light socket. I felt like I was in a war zone with people shooting at us from every direction, but the shooting was coming randomly from the sky.

I had just pulled my dog out of an irrigation ditch filled with water and was sliding down an incline squatting when lightning struck. All I saw was a ball of light surrounding me, and for a moment everything stopped.

I was overcome with peace and bliss and an expansive love that was more profound than anything I had ever felt before. It was beyond any earthly experience. Everything paused for a significant moment, and I was lifted from fear, from anxiety, and from every emotion other than love. I did not feel my body, but I did sense my soul like I was a part of something greater than me.

And then my roommate grabbed me and yelled, "We have to go!" I snapped back into my body and into life. My whole right side was numb and my liver felt like it had been stabbed with a knife. Everything around me was so fast-paced and intense after that profound moment. Some inner part of me picked myself up and made it through a metal fence, across an open field, and back to the safety of my house. We were alive! It was a miracle.

I was in my third week of massage school when this happened, and the next day when I went to class, everyone was checking in about their weekend. People were talking about parties they had been to and the lighthearted things they had done.

When it got to me I said, "I got struck by lightning." The room went silent.

The teacher asked if she could work on me and while she did, my body released so much heat that the room temperature went up fifteen degrees. I think the treatment saved me from some of the long-term side effects of the lightning.

It took me a long time to recover from that much energy in my body. As I integrated it, I became more capable of helping people heal and also more capable of supporting people as they processed life and death.

A couple of years later, I had another near-death experience.

I was driving to meet a good friend for her son's birthday party at an Italian restaurant. It was pouring rain outside, it was rush hour, and it was dark.

I was in a left-turn lane, cars whizzing by me, when a car opposite me going about 40 miles an hour came into my lane and hit me head-on. My car was pushed back with a massive force but my body stayed still, so my seatbelt felt like it was crushing my heart. When it happened, my whole being exploded in light. I saw a giant ball of light surround my heart and was aware of the same bliss and love and peace I had experienced with the lightning strike.

Again, everything stopped. There was a weighted pause filled with love and bliss, and then life started happening around me again.

I was in the middle of the street, and miraculously my car had been knocked straight back so I wasn't hit by any other car. I was able to pull off the road, even though my car was totaled. A retired policeman witnessed the accident and helped me. I ended up being okay, other than some extensive injuries from the seatbelt and from whiplash.

Mom picked me up after my accident and I described what I had experienced to her.

Again, I had "seen the light" and felt a deep knowing that death was not something to fear, but something that was beautiful when the time came.

I didn't feel a loss of self in the moment of "death"; I felt an expansion into more of me and more of life. It was like a window that I didn't know was there opened, and I got a glimpse of something eternal that was always present and always accessible.

What pulled me back were the people and the life I would leave behind. While death felt beautiful and expansive, the life I had here was different but equally powerful and not to be left lightly.

Mom and I talked about the expansive energy I had felt when I came close to death. She was curious and asked lots of questions about what it was like. We explored the realization that death had a lot of light surrounding it. My experiences made us both open our minds to believe that there was more to death than meets the eye, even though there was still a mystery surrounding it and not a complete understanding.

When Mom got the news that her cancer had spread, we revisited these stories while she examined her fears around death.

Beyond my own near-death experiences, Mom and I had the honor to sit with people and animals while they were dying. Mom was with her parents when they died and had lost friends and pets that she loved. I had been with family, clients, friends, and pets during their passing or their dying process.

In the midst of the sadness of loss, there was always a lot of peace and love surrounding the one who was passing. There was an awake energy that felt like a celebration of the life that was lived.

We were both also aware that, while death is hard and sad, it powerfully reminds us to appreciate the time we have here on earth. For almost the whole five years preceding Mom's death, her life was lit up with her proximity to death. Instead of getting lost in the sadness, she and I were often able to connect with the spirit of life that was elevated by the closeness of death.

Life became enhanced with the recognition of the preciousness of self, the connections and love that Mom had established, and the passions and interests that her soul enjoyed in this life. Nothing else mattered.

As illuminated as our days could be, letting go of a life well lived was tragic and was something that had to be felt along the way. Knowing that the light was there helped, but the grief was important for us to sit with as well. Mom had to face death and I had to face losing her.

We had to find the balance of witnessing the beauty of spirit and also acknowledging our human process. Death was both heartbreaking and beautiful. We walked the tightrope walk of both truths with as much grace as we could, but we fell along the way as well.

The light lifted us when we fell and kept us on a path of learning until the end.

Chapter Twelve

Unrelenting Journey to a Treatment

When I think of Mom in connection to her health, I can picture her with her homeopathic medicine, her herbal medicine, her yoga, her mindfulness practices, and also her medications. She blended and embraced both Eastern and Western medicine, and she thought about her health a lot.

Mom was sensitive and aware of her body, and this sensitivity made her a bit of a hypochondriac. Whenever she felt pain, she felt it in a big way. Whenever her blood pressure was off, she would feel it intensely.

A year before she had cancer, she called me one night and told me her tongue was swelling up and she was driving herself to the hospital. When I got in the car to go meet her, she called me and said she was struggling to breathe and then hung up and stopped answering her phone. I was left to drive over there wondering if she was dead. By the time I got there, she was fine, lying in her bed smiling. She had turned off her phone and forgotten to call me and let me know she was okay.

I was used to having a bit of drama around Mom's health.

Mom's sensitivity to her health made her cancer treatment more complex. Of course, her illness would be all-consuming for anyone, but there was an extra edge to it with Mom.

Once we knew Mom had metastatic cancer, the race to find a treatment was on. Since the cancer she had was extremely rare, there was not a lot of research on it. Only one type of treatment, an oral form of chemotherapy, was known to work for Hurthle Cell Carcinoma. Once she started the chemo, it would lose its effectiveness after a couple of years, so it was considered a last resort for her.

The doctors decided to try some clinical trials to see if any of the new and innovative treatments for cancer could work. If a trial medication was successful, it could potentially give Mom a longer life.

Mom loved being in these trials. She liked the thought that what she was doing could help her cancer, but she also enjoyed the fact that the research she was participating in could be impactful for other people who had her type of cancer. Her dad had also loved innovation. He struggled with lung cancer and in the end died of prostate cancer. Mom and her dad were really close.

My dad was a math teacher and a voracious learner. His room at Pulaski High School was number eight and he passed out buttons with that number. He had the complete mathematical division of how to get Pi all around the room. He was an avid reader of non-fiction books and he took the train to and from work and read one book every day. He was always learning.

Mom talked about how Grandpa would have been fascinated by the new developments in cancer medications and how he would have loved that she was on the cutting edge of research.

Clinical trials aren't given in every city, so Mom began a campaign to discover where she would receive her treatment. Luckily Mom was adventurous.

The first trial was in Phoenix and because Aunt Linda lives there, Mom was able to stay with her while she got the trial. I remember driving to Phoenix with Mom, full of hope. We took our time on the drive and stopped in Winslow, Arizona, to have great Mexican food at a restaurant with plastic tablecloths and colorful piñatas and flags adorning the walls. We toasted her new path toward health. If she couldn't totally beat this cancer, at least she could give it a good run for its money.

Phoenix was a place of my childhood. My grandparents lived there until the end of their lives, and I visited them once a year until they died. When Mom was married to my dad, she had been to Phoenix every year, so this was a familiar place for her as well. The fact that Aunt Linda lived there was icing on the cake, because they were great friends and Mom was still adjusting to her robot voice and to all of her different health issues.

When I was little and we went to Phoenix, I always loved it when Grandpa Joe would tell me the story of the phoenix rising from the ashes. The phoenix is a bird that burns up and is reborn from the ashes of its previous life. This felt like an empowered metaphor for Mom and what she was going through. She needed to once again connect with her inner strength, rise from the ashes of her former life, and be reborn an even stronger version of herself.

Well, my adventure continues. I arrived in Phoenix one week ago today and am lucky to be staying with my sister-in-law and her husband, Linda and Jim. They've welcomed me into their home and I feel like one of the family. The weather here is hot, but we venture out for an hour-long walk every morning.

I came here because my doctor at MD Anderson recommended a clinical trial for me that is being done in Scottsdale. I had my first meeting last Tuesday and met with my new doctor who talked with me and Linda for over an hour about how cancers develop, what clinical studies were possibly appropriate for me, and details about how the study would be run.

When we have cancer our genes are literally broken. The gene study done on me at MD Anderson revealed that I have two genes broken, and, at this time, there are unfortunately no treatments to repair those breaks. (Of note, 50 percent of people who develop cancer have one of the same genes broken as I do and there is no treatment for any of us.) But the study that I hope to participate in attempts to cut off what the doctor called the gas pedal that is feeding the cancer.

It's very interesting how it tries to accomplish that. In simple terms, we are first given folic acid or vitamin B9. All cells need folic acid and especially cancer cells. Minutes afterward, the drug is administered and the theory is that the cells will take it because they are gobbling up the folic acid.

I'm having a lovely time in Phoenix, which has grown and changed so much since my children's grandparents moved here and lived here so many years ago. Linda and I have gone to see a play, Vanya and Sonia and Masha and Spike, which won a Tony Award a few years back and was a riot and well-acted, we went to an excellent string quartet concert, and we went to a restaurant we used to go to, Aunt Chiladas. So life continues to be fun if not a bit challenging. I have so much to be thankful for in my life.

I flew out to Phoenix on Thanksgiving for a visit. She and I went all over town exploring, eating good food, shopping for clothes, and drinking cappuccinos. I also got to see the place where she had her treatment. It was filled with courageous souls who were sick and trying to get better. There was a wide mix of attitudes among Mom's fellow patients. Some had brave smiles, some complained bitterly and loudly and were obviously suffering, and some were silent and stoic. Mom was still full of hope.

I always say that I am healthy, I just have cancer. The injection only took one minute, but I was actually at the clinic yesterday with Liz for seven hours because they monitor clients very carefully and have to take a lot of blood draws after the dosage to see how long the medicine stays in my system. The staff was excellent and cheery, but it's difficult to see how many patients there were obviously struggling with their cancer.

Her three-month scan revealed the trial didn't work. Her cancer continued to grow.

Mom adapted to the curveballs her cancer threw at her with a lot of resilience. She would feel momentum and hope with her surgeries and treatments, and then the rug would be pulled out from underneath her and she would be hit by hard news.

Her response was always, "What's my next option?"

Chapter Thirteen

Jimmy Choos and Bucket Lists

The next option was a trial the doctors found for Mom in Seattle, which was a great location because Mike lived there. This began about a month after clearing her body of the previous treatment, so she was able to go there for Christmas and stay.

Christmas was special for Mom and our Seattle family. She traveled there every year for the holiday and was always overjoyed to share all of the traditions with Chris and Abby. They would read tales of Santa and his reindeer, go and look at the lights, bake cookies, and get up early on Christmas morning and open all of the presents. Mom started planning gifts in July, and the anticipation of getting the kids something special that they would remember was always a big deal for her.

Mom adored her grandchildren, so to get to not only share Christmas with them but to also live in the same city was a joyous occasion. As upsetting as it was that her first treatment hadn't worked, she was excited to be with her family.

She moved in with Mike and got ready to start her next trial.

I like my doctor in Seattle a lot; she's honest, but kind and is definitely looking out for my best interests. She's a funky lady who's all dolled up in Jimmy Choo shoes with bright red streaks in her dark black hair. As she enters the room for each of my visits, she lowers her head and peers out at me with her dark eyes, looking closely to see how I'm really doing.

The tumor on her shoulder had become large enough to pinch a nerve, so they decided to do surgery to remove it before she started her next clinical trial.

Since the first trial hadn't worked and her cancer was continuing to spread, Mom's lifespan was uncertain. My brother and I started talking to her about what she would want to do before she died.

There is still joy in my life! When my doctor announced that I could have the needed surgery on the tumor in my shoulder in two days, my first question was, "Can I still go to the championship football game? I'm an avid Packers fan and we have tickets." He told me I could—"Just don't raise that left arm"—and Mike, Kim, Christopher and I went. It was a complete blast. Of course, people couldn't believe that half of our foursome was dressed to support the Seahawks and the other half (me and Mike) were in our Packers gear! Liz was here to babysit for Abby and helped me find a yellow wig, yellow coat, and green boots. It was on my Bucket List to go to another Packers game and I did! OK, so the Packers did lose, but the Seahawks are my second favorite team and I was glad for them.

Through a sea of Seahawks jerseys, Mom walked proud in her crazy outfit. She was fragile but fierce and had no problem getting teased for being a Packers fan. A man came running down the stairs after the Packers lost and hugged Mom and shook everyone's hand and said, "You guys are the classiest fans."

A couple of weeks later, she began her new treatment. The next few months were stressful for Mom and also for Mike and his family.

My family and friends and I are dealing with this as best we can. Mike, Liz, and I went out for dinner one night when Liz was here for a week's visit and we did drink our way through the meal as we talked and laughed and cried about our situation. My friend Loyce was just here for five days and we ventured out on a ferry boat to the San Juan Islands to look for whales. I'll get together with Betty, my nephew Peter, his wife Kira, and their kids Luke and Charlotte soon. If there's one thing I've learned through all of this it is to find joy in each day, and I am lucky to be able to do just that.

I've been continuing to be a gypsy while in Seattle, staying in different places. Most of the time, of course, I've been staying with Mike and Kim and the kids, but have also lived in Kim's mom Jackie's condo when she is out of town, and now have a small apartment in Bellevue nearby donated by the American Cancer Society. The price is a beautiful $13 a day!! Only thing is that I have to check out every weekend so I am still sort of *living out of a suitcase. I will begin looking for a longer-term rental soon, once it looks like the trial is indeed a success.*

It was hard for my family to all live together as much as they did. Mom was still thinking she could live independently. They were all dealing with the realization that Mom needed more support than she wanted to admit, and they were having a difficult time talking with each other about their needs. I was there every three to four weeks to help, and it was becoming more and more of a dilemma to figure out how to sustain what she required mentally, emotionally, and physically.

Change kept happening so quickly. Mom's abilities and her ailments were constantly shifting. It was a daunting task to stay current with her condition so we could tend to her needs and also take care of ourselves along the way.

I drove her car up to her from Albuquerque in the middle of all of this, and then I bought a car in Seattle to drive back home.

I remember sitting in a cafe in the University District in Seattle waiting to meet her for lunch. I waited and waited and then I finally called her. She was in a panic. She was lost and couldn't figure out where she was. Mom was never good with directions, but she had lost her ability to reason through problems and would just freeze. Cell phones back then didn't have the good maps that they have now, and Mom was confused by apps anyway. I finally talked her through it and she settled down and found her way to me, but it was scary for her and also for me. I didn't know if she should be driving. Especially in a busy and big city like Seattle.

Mom kept me company on part of my drive to Albuquerque in my new car. She needed to be back in Seattle for her treatment after a couple of days, so she rode with me to Salt Lake City and then flew home. While we drove, we talked and talked and had lots of laughs. Being on long car rides was a part of my relationship with Mom. She loved road trips and was at home on the road almost more than she was anywhere else.

If you ask me to picture Mom, I would immediately picture her in her car, sunglasses on, windows rolled down, a great big smile on her face ready for her next adventure. Her desire to explore started at an early age.

> I was a little rebel all of my life and a little independent "cuss." My mom and I would get into hassles a lot because I didn't want to do what she wanted me to do. I ran away from home three or four times when I was little.
>
> One time when we lived in Brookdale, Wisconsin, my mom looked out the window just in time to see me going up over the hill with my suitcase and my dog Timmie on a leash. I was about three years old.
>
> Another time, I packed my Mary Jane shoes in my suitcase and marched down the street. My mom caught me and made me sit in a chair for the rest of the day.

Before Mom moved to Albuquerque in the late nineties, she took a six-week camping trip around the Southwest. This was before cell phones, which is unimaginable now. I remember getting messages on my answering machine from her on her travels. Her voice was always filled with inspiration from all of the beautiful sights she had seen and people she had met that day.

On this final road trip from Seattle with me, she drove maybe an hour out of the trip. It didn't make me any less concerned about her driving. We stopped at a grocery store and she nearly hit a car on the way out of the parking lot. I had to monitor and backseat drive the whole hour she was behind the wheel. I knew in my heart that I was going to have to talk with her about whether or not she should drive, and I knew that when she stopped being able to drive, she would be devastated.

We watched the Academy Awards on our last night of the trip and enjoyed looking at the dresses and seeing all of the fashion. This was one of our favorite things to do together, but I could feel that we both had a lot on our minds, and the joy of it was a little less amplified.

I dropped her off at the Salt Lake City airport so she could fly back to Seattle. As I took the highway toward Albuquerque, I felt unsettled and concerned about the road to come for Mom.

A week later, she broke her hip.

She never drove again.

Chapter Fourteen

Shattered and Reborn

While in her clinical trial, Mom was active and walked every day. One day while she was staying at her apartment in Bellevue, she was on a walk near her hotel. She felt something pop in her hip, followed by an excruciating pain. She didn't fall, but she couldn't move because of the pain and was frozen in place.

When this happened, Mom had not brought her talking stick and she panicked. She couldn't call for help and once again—she couldn't move.

She was on the sidewalk on a busy street so she started waving her arms and mouthing, "HELP."

Nobody stopped. People just drove by and didn't bother to help. Mom was in agony and no one came to her aid.

She was there for what felt like an eternity to her but in reality was about a half an hour until finally a man pulled over and came tentatively toward her. He wouldn't get close to her and she couldn't talk to tell him what was wrong. I'm sure she looked wild because she was panicked and needed help, but I am equally sure she looked frail and harmless.

The man called the police and a police officer came.

They finally understood Mom's pantomimed attempt to say that she couldn't talk and gave her some paper to write on. By then, she was in a full-on panic attack and was also in agony from a broken hip.

The police officer somehow got her into his car, and she wrote her hotel down and he just dropped her off there. He didn't help her to the lobby, and he didn't help her to her room. He just let her out at the front door and drove off.

I have no idea how Mom got help. Someone gave her an office chair with wheels and she pushed herself to her own room where she called Kim, who took her to the hospital. There it was discovered that the hip had cancer in it and had fractured while she was out walking.

This was one of the devastating moments of her journey. The way it happened, the lack of support, and the agony of feeling all alone were profound.

It was clear that Mom's treatment was not working. Her cancer was progressing and eating away at her bones, causing them to weaken and break. Mom was in the hospital for a week and went to a rehab center afterward. In order to strengthen her bones, they did radiation treatments on the cancer inside her hip and also on her shoulder.

Finished my radiation treatments, and it's still not clear if they were successful or not. I do feel that I have less discomfort in my right arm, but the pain in my right hip remains. This cancer of mine is a stubborn one; it turns out that only

1 percent of people with thyroid cancer have my kind of cancer and my doctor has only treated one other person with it. (I always knew I was a rare bird but why, oh, why did I have to get this rarity?) I'm also fully aware that there is no cure for my cancer; all we can hope for is to keep it at bay. Luckily, so far I haven't had many side effects, just fatigue and a deep achy feeling as if I have the flu.

While Mom was at the rehab center, she fell into a bit of despair. The place was filled with people who had some kind of severe trauma. Even without the ability to smell well, Mom said it stunk.

I remember talking with her on the phone while she was there, and I could hear the sadness, even in her robot voice. Her words were long and drawn out and sorrowful. She felt alone and lonely. She was facing potentially never driving again because of her broken hip. She was going to have to start using a walker. She couldn't talk, and now she could barely walk. She was shattered.

Losing the ability to drive was extremely difficult for Mom. Eating. Talking. And now driving. What was there left to live for?

Well, my challenges continue, but I'm still finding reasons to have fun and enjoy a laugh or two or three or four. Still using a walker (actually I have two walkers since I'm now living at Mike and Kim's again and have one for each level of the house). My granddaughter Abby and my grandson Christopher have continued to put stickers on one of them (a mixture of robots, princesses, flowers, Dr. Seuss, and pictures of one of my favorite "hunks," Han Solo in Star Wars) and they so, so sweetly help me go up and down the stairs with *my flowered cane. I really miss driving around by myself, but, hopefully, that day will once again arrive.*

On my next visit to Seattle, I was greeted with a mom with a big smile and a highly decorated walker. She was wearing it with style.

Somehow in the midst of despair, Mom had connected with her inner light and spirit and decided to live. This was not the first time I had seen her find her strength and it wasn't the last time. Every time she did, though, I was in awe of her.

She lost so much, but with every physical aspect of life she lost, she gained momentum in connecting with an inner force that activated the conscious desire to live.

What I saw awakening along the way with Mom was gratitude. It's not that Mom was ungrateful before, but just like all of us, she came to take things for granted.

When cancer stole Mom's ability to take *anything* for granted, Mom had to be grateful for what she did have. Or I guess the other alternative for her was to turn into an angry and sad person. Thank goodness she took the path of gratitude.

She did have moments where she felt despair. There were so many times she had to let the latest crushing news wash over her. She lost her voice and her sense of taste and smell. She lost her ability to laugh out loud and her ability to cry out loud. She lost her ability to walk well and occasionally lost her ability to walk at all. She lost her ability to drive. Her cancer kept spreading. She continued to need more chemo and radiation.

So many people asked me, "What does your mom have to live for?"

So many people told me, "If it were me, I wouldn't want to live."

Strange things for people to say, but Mom saw the essence of life itself as worthwhile.

Being alive. Period. Was worth it.

Seeing a sunset, seeing her daughter, son, sister, grandkids, family, friends, and random strangers laugh and smile. Having one more conversation about fashion or books or movies. Meeting one more interesting person. Eating one more awesome meal. All of these little things and more became amplified and important for Mom.

She did not take one moment for granted.

What Mom found in all of this was a love for life itself. The very breath we breathe and the world we live in became divine for her. Being around her, being in her presence, would awaken that feeling of a divine moment in people.

Mom's metamorphosis was contagious, and the brilliant butterfly that had emerged was becoming more visible day by day.

Chapter Fifteen

Purpose

There was one thing Mom would get stuck on.

"What is my purpose?" she would ask and she would really be open to digging in and exploring that question.

I told her that I felt like she was embodying her purpose by getting out into the world and shining her unique light.

After her massive surgery, it was hard to comprehend how she was alive, let alone smiling and laughing and enjoying life. She didn't cower or hide; she went out and talked to everyone she met, whether they understood her or not. She took every opportunity she could to explore life, and she let everyone see her.

The fact that she was so brave challenged and changed so many people's lives.

Mom's teaching was really that she loved life, no matter what. Whether her bones were breaking from the cancer, whether she was sick from her medications, whether she couldn't walk very well or drive, she was still inspired to live.

Mom lived from a place of enthusiasm, getting out and exploring life without the barriers some people have. Some people might think they were too old or too jaded, but Mom ignored all of that and took on life with enthusiasm. She looked at herself as a brand-new person every day.

I felt like her strength and bravery served an important purpose in the world, and I expressed this to her.

"But what can I *do* to feel like I have purpose?" she would ask.

Mom communicated that her purpose before she had cancer had been wrapped up in her profession, in her writing, and in her conversations with people.

When she got cancer, a lot of that had stopped. Although she could still write, she could not think as clearly, so even that became hard.

I asked her if she thought *doing* was what purpose was about.

Being an English teacher, she had us look up the definition of purpose. The basic definition is: the reason for which something is done. By definition, purpose is not *what* we do. Purpose is the motivation, the reason *why* we do anything.

Even though Mom could not do as much on a physical level, she could still feel purpose in her life. She could still find motivation from within and let her heart be filled with inspiration.

Mom's purpose emanated from her unbridled enjoyment of life, and she seemed to slowly understand that her identity came from that deeper place. If she came from a place of love and gratitude, then it didn't matter as much if she could not do something.

I saw a shift in her understanding of purpose in the relationships she had at the end of her life. Most people who spent time with Mom told me how much light and good energy she had brought them.

One of Mom's important motivations that impacted me immeasurably was the purpose of being a mother.

Mike and I were lucky beyond words to have her in our lives, and she embodied an ideal mother. There were times she fell, but she learned and grew in this purpose throughout her life. She loved us unconditionally, even when we were incredibly dumb, and was always there for us. We got what we deserved, whether it was tough love or soft love or somewhere in between. There was not a time in our lives that we lived without her support, even though there were times that she asked us to grow and was "disappointed" in us.

Chris and Abby got to see the incredible purpose of the grandmother in Mom and felt the unconditional love from her that will remain in their hearts throughout their lives. Part of the reason Mom lived as spectacularly and as long as she did was because she wanted her grandkids to know her and to remember the love she had for them. Whether they remember the specifics of who she was, I know that her love for them made an indelible impression on their souls.

At the end of her life, Mom had to turn a lot of her authority over to Mike and me so that we could be there for her. It was not easy on any of us, but I can see that it was a rite of passage for Mike and me as her children. As she was leaving this life, we needed to step into our potential more so that we could truly let her go. She passed the baton over slowly and we took it reluctantly, but she served the purpose of mother by making sure we were empowered in ourselves before she left.

By the time Mom died, she embodied gratitude and love. She realized that doing was not really what purpose was about. She was mother and grandmother, she was bold, she was brave, she was vibrant, she was loving, and she was grateful. By personifying all of those beautiful ways of being, she felt purpose alive in her life.

Chapter Sixteen

The Tale of Two Cities

After Mom broke her hip, it became more and more clear that it was a struggle for Mike and his family to juggle taking care of their kids and also taking care of Mom.

Since the trials were not working, her team of doctors decided to put her on the chemotherapy that was known to help with her cancer. She was able to take this chemo anywhere, unlike the trials she had been on, so she had the possibility of moving back to Albuquerque.

Even before she had cancer, Mom was torn between living near me and being near Mike and Kim and the kids. She had moved to Seattle for a year when Chris was two and had enjoyed being there, but she had trouble making ends meet. When she moved back to Albuquerque, a part of her heart stayed in Seattle with Mike. Every summer she would take the long drive to Washington State and stay for at least a month. She loved Mike and me so thoroughly that she felt ambiguous about where to be.

At this point in her journey, her body was breaking down at a rapid pace. Cancer can be brutal when it starts to win. It feels like you're trying to hold water in your hands, and it's pouring through your fingers beyond your control.

Mom needed radiation on two tumors on her head that had grown large. The radiation caused her a lot of nausea and confusion. She kept forgetting to drink liquids, so she wound up in the hospital for severe dehydration.

This was the first of many trips to the hospital for this reason.

With severe dehydration, it is a little confusing to understand what is going on. In the initial stages, it seemed like she was a little drunk and disoriented. As it got worse, she would start to talk gibberish and slur her words and look really lethargic. At that point it would mimic a stroke. It was especially bewildering with Mom because she talked with a robot voice and most people would not notice that her speech was off.

I finished my round of ten radiation treatments and this run was a bit rougher than the other one. Had some serious nausea and a bit of vomiting, so it was more uncomfortable than the first round. Maybe that was because it was on my head? Medication did help, so that's good.

As of now, I am also having some hair loss and my doctor informed me it will be permanent. Maybe I'd better start looking for some smashingly good-looking hats? Two of the spots are pretty red, and I do have one bald spot near the larger spot. I talk and look like an alien now! Ha!

I started my chemo again after five days, but maybe that was a bit too soon, because one night I got really sick, with

serious diarrhea and incontinence all night and then disori-
entation the next day. Called the doctor and, to make a long
story short, ended up in the hospital for almost a week.
Liz flew in to help me out and the diagnosis: severe
dehydration.

Mom had started to have "chemo brain," which was the fog in
the brain that came from the medicines she took. It made her less
capable of finding her words and keeping cohesive thoughts. This
made everyday life very difficult

When I flew out to be with Mom, we realized that her need for help
was too great and that she would need to move into an independent
living facility. This was not an easy decision for her. She had resisted
these places because she felt like she was giving up on life by moving
there. She loved her independence, and while these places are called
"independent" living, they come into your life precisely when you
start to lose your ability to be independent. They have meals for you
and they have shuttles to take you where you need to go.

We talked with the social worker at the hospital and found Mom
a place near Mike and Kim, and she was transferred there from the
hospital.

Mom embraced this new living situation with a brave heart. There
was a one-hundred-year-old woman named Grace who lived at her
facility, and Mom and she fell into a friendship. People struggled with
understanding her, but she pushed through the social challenges with
a positive attitude.

As much as she liked her temporary home, she still needed a
huge amount of assistance that Mike and Kim were struggling to
give, because they had a family to take care of as well. She needed

help with phone calls, prescriptions, tracheostomy care, and multiple doctor's appointments. With her chemo brain and constantly changing life, she needed a lot of emotional support as well. Mom's care was a full-time job. Just the doctor's appointments alone were crazy. She had physical therapy, speech therapy, weekly meetings with her oncologist, radiation therapy, a heart doctor and more. There were so many aspects of her health to juggle.

Through talking with Mom, it seemed potentially better for her to return to Albuquerque so that I could help her. I had more space in my life to support her growing needs. I told her to talk with Mike and we could all figure it out together.

I flew out with my friend Annie for Mom's birthday with the intention of driving Mom's car home because she could not drive and she no longer needed it. We could also possibly move some of her things back to Albuquerque, depending on what she and Mike discussed.

When Annie and I got to Seattle, we found out that Mom had not shared anything with Mike. She knew she needed more help, but she was devastated to leave her family. Sometimes when Mom felt those big emotions she became paralyzed and unable to communicate. It was an emotional visit for all of us, but we got through it.

I pause here to ponder how to describe the family dynamics for all of us at this time. We were all under the strain of knowing that Mom was dying. We were all under the strain of the constant and quick loss of function that Mom was going through. We were all struggling with the fact that Mom had been incredibly independent and now was incredibly dependent. We all had lives that were going on when this massive curveball called cancer had been thrown at us.

None of us dealt with it perfectly.

It caused stress and strain on all of us for five years of our lives, and that caused tension at times between us. We all handle situations like this differently. In the overall picture, we all loved each other and did the best we could for each other and for ourselves. I had the openness in my life because I didn't have kids. No one but Mom was dependent on me, so it made sense that she should be near me.

It made sense, but that didn't make it easy. Mom had to leave her son, her daughter-in-law, her grandkids, and that choice was shattering for her. When she left, she knew she would see them, but she would not get to be in their day-to-day lives anymore.

Annie and I drove Mom's car and stuff back to Albuquerque, and she took a flight to New Mexico a week later. I did not get to see my family's goodbyes, but I am sure they were filled with a lot of tears. Mom entered yet another phase of her journey.

I realized today how many different places I have lived in the past six months: Phoenix with Linda and Jim, Seattle with Mike and Kim, two different hospitals, a rehabilitation/ nursing home, an independent living facility, and now back to Albuquerque. Yikes! It's hard to believe that so much has happened to me in such a short time. I feel lucky that I've had so many people who love and support me.

She had come full circle and was back where it all began.

Chapter Seventeen

Home to the Familiar and the New

Before Mom got to Albuquerque, some friends and I moved all of her stuff from storage into her new independent living apartment. We wanted her to feel at home, and we wanted her to get to see the things that she loved.

It was a bit surreal to move her into this place. It was an old-fashioned facility, and the dining room looked like a supper club from the fifties. We wheeled her furniture through the halls on dollies, passing colorless pictures on pastel walls. The place smelled like perfumed lavender hand lotion. As hard as it was for Mom to move to a place like this, it was also strange for me to imagine her there.

There were only two sloth-like elevators, and Mom was moving to the third floor. Somehow, my friends and I timed our move right after lunch was over. The entire facility needed the elevator at the same time we did.

It was quite the introduction to the world of independent living. Everyone stubbornly pushed their walkers in front of us, wanting to know who we were and what we were doing. If we had a time frame when it came to moving, it became obvious that we wouldn't be able to adhere to it.

Mom would not be able to hide in this new living situation, and everyone would know her business sooner than later.

We maneuvered through walkers, canes, fragile people, and slow elevators, and it took us forever to get all of her stuff to her new home. Her eclectic furniture and art brightened the hallways for a moment and transformed her mundane room into a wealth of treasures from around the globe. An oasis that felt like Mom; I breathed a sigh of relief.

I know we are not our things, but there is definitely an identity in the furniture we pick and in the artwork and objects we surround ourselves with.

Mom was going to have to adjust to a new apartment where they cooked her food for her, where they ate communal meals, and where there were all new people to get to know. At least she could have her own space that reflected her colorful self.

When I brought her from the airport, she looked a little shell-shocked when she walked through the front doors into the dining room and saw the pastel walls and sterile environment. I could see her straightening her shoulders and taking a deep breath in an attempt to be positive.

When she got to her room that was adorned with vibrant color and her own furniture and art, her whole demeanor changed and she relaxed. Home.

"This is awesome," she said.

Mission accomplished: We had created a smooth transition.

Mom had moved many times since she left the house I grew up in. Each time she moved, she whittled down her possessions, so that by the time she got to her new apartment she was left with the objects that were most important to her.

The two things that stand out to me that immediately make me think of Mom are her Persian rug and her reading chair.

The Persian rug was a huge purchase for Mom back when I was a child. There was a rug store Mom loved near our house in Madison, Wisconsin. We would walk there and she would spend hours looking through the rugs and talking to the owners. I was always bored to tears, but I can still recall the smell of the place. It was the smell of wool and almost, but not quite, the smell of dirty barn animals.

The rugs at this store were high quality and expensive and, on a teacher's salary, Mom had to save her money for many months to be able to afford one. She grew up in the Depression era and was not a spender, so this was a huge purchase for her. All the patterns of the rugs were beautiful, and finally she chose one that she loved. It had a playful design with animals and geometric shapes throughout, and it was orange and rich with a mix of vibrant colors.

We brought the rug home and immediately my dog Huckle threw up on it. It was funny later, but Mom was pretty devastated at the time. It had to be cleaned professionally, so she had to take it straight back to the store. Huckle was in trouble for a long time after that, but Mom got her rug back and loved it for the rest of her life.

By the time the rug got to her apartment, it had traveled far and was faded and tattered around the edges, but it was still beautiful.

I don't remember where or how Mom got her chair, but I remember her having it reupholstered when I was a child, so she had it over forty years. She took a lot of care picking the fabric, and she chose colors that blended with her rug. It became her main chair to sit in and to read or watch television.

It wound up being too low for her to sit in because of her hip issues, but she was happy to have it in her new place for guests. It was familiar and a reminder of home.

Mom settled into her new life with a little resistance but also with a brave heart and a sense of adventure.

She would text me while she was at dinner, "The man across from me is asleep at the table." "The blind guy walked into a wall." "No one can understand me because everyone here is deaf." "A guy kissed me on the way to lunch." "Somebody tell a joke."

She had a sense of humor about it all.

The most stressful thing initially for Mom was the man who reacted badly to her robot voice. He came up to Mom during their evening meal and started yelling at her to shut up, and he got pretty aggressive with her. A person at Mom's table stepped between them, but it was a bad scene.

It really frightened Mom because she was so frail and she couldn't respond to him. She had to use her robot voice to say anything, and her voice was what was making him so angry.

Thank goodness the person at her table intervened and saved the day, but the man would not stop being hostile with Mom. It turned out that he had cognitive issues and couldn't understand that Mom was talking. He just thought she was making the robot noise for no reason.

Mom handled the situation with a lot of courage. On her own, she talked with the administrators of her facility. She had a disability and they needed to honor her and support her with it. They finally had the man removed to a nursing home that had memory care, but it was a rough way to begin in a new living situation.

Our next step after settling into her apartment was to establish a new doctor for her treatment.

We really got lucky because Mom's doctor in Seattle referred us to an oncologist in Albuquerque who also worked in palliative care. Palliative care supports people with life-threatening illnesses. It helps the patients deal with their diagnosis, and it also helps their families juggle the difficulties of navigating treatment and care.

Her new doctor had extra knowledge and compassion for Mom and me and what we were going through, and she recommended that we get established with the palliative care department of the hospital, which we did. This turned out to be very important for Mom's future.

We walked into my appointment with my doctor to find out the results of a CT scan following the new dose of chemotherapy. We were getting the news about whether or not it was working. I've been through this scenario several times of course, and it's always a nerve-wracking experience. We'd had our hopes up this time, though, because a couple of my tumors on the surface had disappeared, so when I saw my doctor in an office up ahead and she gave us a big, bright smile, I was thinking, "Can the news really be good?"

And, sure enough, the news is very good! All of my tumors have reduced in size, both the fast- and slow-growing ones, so we are all very happy indeed. I can be on this chemo indefinitely, and there are two other possible drugs for me, so that is good as well. I have to keep in mind that there's no cure for my cancer; we can just hope to keep it at bay and that's what I'm wishing for. And that I can tolerate the dose.

For the next year, Mom had a few hospital visits for severe dehydration from the chemo, but her cancer itself continued to shrink and she was able to live a fragile but good existence.

We went to monthly appointments, she had scans every three months, and we found some kind of rhythm. In the meantime, the cancer was looming and we chose to live as large as we could.

We met her grandkids and Mike and Kim at Disneyland, another experience she had on her bucket list. Her wheelchair got us to the front of every line and she loved making us VIPs. We all laughed and celebrated life together.

At this point Mom stopped writing about her cancer and immersed herself in living for the rest of her days.

Chapter Eighteen

Conversations with Mom

I would bust Mom out of her independent living facility as often as I could, and I found myself carving out space in my schedule to be available for fun.

When I would pick Mom up, she would be outside with a sweet smile on her face waiting for me. I tried to memorize the image.

She stood there leaning on her walker, hip cocked, always owning whatever style had inspired her in the day. Often she wore clothes that didn't match, but that somehow worked on her. A wild electric-blue shirt, with crazily patterned colorful capris and slip-on shoes adorned her elegant but frail body. Her signature baseball cap was on her head to cover her tumors, and her pink hair was peeking out at all angles underneath.

There were people outside talking with her occasionally, but she always lit up when I pulled the car around and marched straight for me as though nothing else mattered to her as much as our time together.

There was such joy awaiting both of us when we gathered. The anticipation of conversations, good food, and exploring was always felt between the two of us as I hugged her, loaded her walker in the car, and got her situated in the front seat.

I would begin to drive before she got her talker out of her purse, and then her robot voice would be awake and alive and we would dig into the day's conversations.

One time Mom said to me, "I could talk to you all day, every day; I love talking to you that much." I felt the same way about her. We would laugh about stupid things. We would dissect situations and relationships. We would talk movies, fashion, and books. We would tell stories of our lives multiple times in multiple ways. We would consider the divine, our souls, and the universe. We were never bored with each other.

Mom and I had a quirky dynamic. I saved some text conversations she and I had.

"Just wanted to thank you for driving me all over town lately. You're a peach."

"You're welcome, Mamacita! You're worth all of the gold in China. I love you."

"I love you too. You're the cat's pajamas."

"I will smell like roses this afternoon. I'm having a shower."

"Wheee!"

"I've been listening to your YouTube videos about intuition and learning a lot. Wondering how to ground myself. Can you do more videos about how to do that?"

"Will do! Great idea."

"Please cancel my acupuncture appointment for Thursday. And do it tonight. Ha!"

"Aye Aye, Captain."

"Ahoy matey!"

"See you in the Himalayas tonight. Love you."

"Yes, meet you in our dreams. Love you."

"Good morning to you. I had dreams about me, Phil, Kevin, and Sherry going around Madison at night to clubs. What were your dreams?"

"I had flying dreams!"

"Can't wait to compare notes."

"You have an appointment at the orthopedic doctor tomorrow at 1:10."

"Thanks."

"You did good daughter."

"I love you to the moon and back Elizabeth Sara Vance."

"I love you to the moon and back too Mamacita. Sweet dreams."

Chapter Nineteen

Drinking In Life

One of the adventures Mom and I went on frequently in New Mexico was to go to see the snow geese and sandhill cranes at the Bosque del Apache National Wildlife Refuge. A wetland surrounded by mountains south of Albuquerque, its landscapes mirrored the paintings of Georgia O'Keefe. The unique light of New Mexico created shadows and depth in the terrain and illuminated vibrant clouds in the cobalt-blue skies.

Thousands of birds migrate to this spectacular refuge every year for the winter. Sandhill cranes live in Wisconsin in the summer, so we always felt a special kinship to our feathered friends that lived in New Mexico and our home state of Wisconsin.

At times there were thousands of birds on the ground, and they would all take off simultaneously to the sky in an awe-inspiring chorus of sound and vision. We could hear the wind in their wings, and we would feel an uplifting of energy. Not only was this beautiful, but it also made our whole being return to a place where everything was possible.

On our hour-and-a-half drive to the Bosque, we talked about everything. Epic road trips were a part of my family's culture, and we laughed about the journeys we took. Mom loved to reminisce about a cross-country trek that she and her sister had taken with her parents when they were little.

They had traveled in a Woodie station wagon for thirteen weeks from Wisconsin to California and back, exploring and camping along the way. They would land at a campsite at night, and all the kids would gather around their car as they pulled up. Aunt Betty and Mom had instant friends to play with for the day or two they would stay.

My grandfather was a fly fisherman, and he would go fishing while the family would hang out and play in the streams and enjoy engaging with people and landscapes.

In addition to being a fly fisherman and teacher, my grandfather was a carpenter, and he was always building things. He had designed a car-top carrier so they could pack all their clothes and belongings for the months they would be gone.

In the morning, he would climb up on the car and each person would call out to him what they needed from the storage space.

"Diana, underpants, shorts, shirt!"

He would go to the box labeled Diana and get her stuff. Mom was so impressed with her dad for coming up with such a great organization system.

She and Aunt Betty slept in the front of the car and her parents slept in the back. Mom talked about this fondly as a cozy arrangement.

We had a very special car called a "Woodie" station wagon that had real wood and my dad would have to treat it by

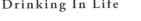

sanding and varnishing it. I felt like a queen riding in this car, and I could spread out in the back seat with my sister. All four of us slept in this on our thirteen-week trip.

One night we could hear a car horn blowing in the campground and we thought it would never stop. Then we realized that it was our horn blowing! We had a piece of wood across the two front seats so we could sleep up there, and it had gotten lodged under the horn and made it blow. We laughed and laughed about that.

Tires were not built well like the tires we have now, and the roads were not as good either; freeways and highways were dreams for the future back then. They had to carry around two spare tires and had to change them frequently and then restock along the way.

Credit cards did not exist, either, so they had to carry the money they needed with them. They ran out of money in California and had to have Mom's grandparents wire them cash in order to get home.

I could tell from the way Mom told the stories from their travels that every trial her family encountered along the way was approached with a sense of humor. I can imagine there was stress along the way for my grandma and grandpa, but it didn't ever come across in her tales of the journey, and on some levels the mishaps seemed like the best part for her.

The spirit of making lemonade from lemons lived strong in Mom and is inherent in me as well.

Mom continued to desire great adventures. This early journey for her was just the beginning of a lifelong fascination with the open road.

When I was a kid, both my mom and my dad were teachers, so we all had the summers off. This created the space for legendary trips. Every other year we drove east and every other year we drove west. We explored cities and we explored the country with equal gusto.

A funny story from one of our trips was very different from the tales of my grandfather's organizational skills. We went to New York City in a rust-colored Chevy Citation that had one of those carriers on the top of our car that looked like a hamburger. It was a cringeworthy get-up for Mike and me.

Unlike Grandpa, Dad did not pack well, and we put our clothes and travel gear into big black trash sacks and pillowcases. We pulled up to the nice apartment in Manhattan that some of Mom's friends lived in. The doorman came out to greet us and Dad opened the "hamburger." Out poured our trash bags, pillow cases, random shoes, and as many embarrassing items as you can imagine onto the street.

It's a funny story now. As a teenager, not so much.

Toward the end of Mom's life it was only fitting that we made it a priority to do road trips. Mom's health was such that the road trips turned mostly into day trips, and so we went to the Bosque del Apache Wildlife Refuge often, as well as to Santa Fe to see art, landscapes, thrift shops, and to eat good food; Jemez Springs, to spend the day exploring a dormant volcano; Fourth of July Canyon in the Manzano Mountains to see the trees vibrant with fall colors; Bandelier, to wander around a National Monument with cliff dwellings; and the mountains near Albuquerque to look at breathtaking vistas.

Every time we went out touring, we got to see a new side of life. Talking to people on her travels had always been important to Mom. After losing her voice, she became more focused on the beauty of the landscapes and the conversations she and I could have along the way.

"It's sooooo beautiful," was something that she expressed many times in the last few years of her life.

A simple sunset, a simple cloud, a simple bird could inspire an expansive feeling of beauty for Mom at the end of her life. She drank it in like someone thirsty from crossing the desert.

Just like her parents, she didn't shy away from a problem that could create an interesting experience. One time, we were at a place called Bernardo Fields, which is near Bosque del Apache. The cranes and snow geese spend winters there as well. It was the night of the full moon, and we were meeting friends to watch it rise on the horizon at sunset.

We stopped at a bathroom and got back into the car. I turned the ignition and my car wouldn't start. I opened the hood and saw that the battery had corroded and its wire was unattached to the engine. We were in the middle of nowhere.

Serendipitously, a bunch of people began to pull into the same parking lot. This lot was normally empty, and it filled up like there was a party. I guess we were the party. Mom was never shy to ask for help, and soon we were surrounded by people wondering what was needed. Our friends showed up and smiled at the support Mom naturally attracted.

Within minutes, our group figured out a solution for what seemed to me like an impossible task. A man was able to jerry-rig my car to start with a pair of pliers that held the wires together, but we couldn't turn off the engine or it would not restart. We were going to have to cross our fingers that the pliers held and drive it straight home to my mechanic.

We waved goodbye to our friends and drove back in a little bit of shock and awe that a solution to our problem had appeared as suddenly and miraculously as it had.

What could have been annoying and a little nerve-wracking turned out to be something fun and filled with laughter. We smiled with gratitude the whole way home thinking of all the people who had come to our aid and how much like Mom's dad a lot of them had been. Grandpa Ken was a tinkerer and a puzzler and would have been the one to figure out what to do, just like the man who saved us that day.

Even though Grandpa hadn't physically been with us, he was with us in spirit, and we were convinced that he brought all of those people to the parking lot in the middle of nowhere to fix our car so we weren't stranded.

We got home safe and sound.

While we went on our day trips, Mom would inevitably need a nap. She survived cancer as long as she did partly from divine luck and partly because she tended to and listened to her body well. Between the chemo and the cancer, she got tired and needed to sleep at least once a day, and the rest seemed to rejuvenate her and set her back on track.

While she slept, I would go out and hike. Just like she needed a nap to survive and thrive, I needed to move around and see beautiful things to balance all of the caregiving I did. The one thing that soothed me and kept me going was to explore the landscapes of New Mexico, breathe fresh air, and take in the majesty of this planet.

I tried to time my walks so she would have a good nap but not be awake and bored before I got back. When she got bored, she could become restless and get out of the car and wander a bit. Because she wasn't steady on her feet, that could be a disaster.

One day she fell when I was with her and it was like a tree fall-ing—she just fell over, her arms and legs straight like a board. We were in a parking lot; a few women witnessed it with me and we all were too late to break her fall. She hit a curb and was bleeding a little bit on her arm. Luckily she was okay, which was a miracle for someone who had bones that could easily break from the cancer in them. Even though she wasn't injured that time, I did not want to repeat the experience.

When I returned to the car from my adventures, Mom wanted to know all the details of where I went and what I saw.

Occasionally she would want to wander a bit with me, and between her wheelchair, her scooter, and her walker, we would find a way for her to come along.

During a visit to Bandelier, I pushed her wheelchair through a visitor center filled with people and tight corners. Once outside, we traversed rough pavement to get to a place where she could see the cliff dwellings. It was always a bit of a workout on my part, but it was also always worth it in the end because she would be filled with gratitude and appreciation when we got somewhere special.

"It's soooooo beautiful."

"It's soooooo amazing."

"Thank you soooooo much."

At one point, some of my cousins came to say goodbye to Mom. This was their last time seeing my mom, and it was a sweet and also somewhat weighted moment. Aunt Betty came with them to spend time with everyone and so did Mike and Kim and the kids.

Mom chose to stay at the hotel where they were all staying in order to be close and not miss any of the action. I was getting into my car to drive home, and I saw Mom come out of her room. She just stood there looking peaceful.

I walked back her way and asked if she was okay.

"I'm just drinking it in," she said.

There was not a particularly good view from this hotel. It faced a parking lot.

"Drinking it in?" I asked.

She took a deep breath and said, "Drinking in life." She seemed so serene and peaceful, and I just stood there drinking in life with her.

Chapter Twenty

Pink Bunnies and Ghosts

While my cousin Tibi, his wife Lia, and their kids Jaden and Tristan were visiting, we all took a drive to a ghost town in New Mexico called Madrid. Since death was close for Mom and ghosts were on our mind, we all began telling ghost stories. The game was to guess which story really happened and which we had made up.

I began. The first time I encountered a ghost, it completely changed my perception of life.

I had just graduated from the University of Wisconsin and had moved to New Mexico with a college friend. Two buddies from school came out to visit me, and we were all driving around seeing the sights of this incredible state where I now lived.

We had gone to Santa Fe and were driving the backroads home to Albuquerque so we could get out and see the stars along the way. There are two ghost towns along the windy drive home; one is called Cerrillos and the other Madrid. I was driving and having an animated conversation with my friend in the front seat with me. Our other friends were sleeping in the back.

All of a sudden, I turned a corner and my headlights picked up a large man in the middle of the road in front of me. There was no time to swerve, and I braked really hard but hit him full-on going 50 miles per hour. My friend and I screamed.

There was no impact. We went right through him.

My car came to a full stop; we looked behind us and no one was there.

"Did you see that guy?" I asked my friend in the front seat.

"Totally," she said.

"But I didn't hit him! I went right through him," I said.

"That is so crazy!"

We had, of course, woken up our friends in the back, and they were wondering what we were screaming about.

"I think we just saw a ghost," I said.

At this point, we just wanted to get out of there. We were in the middle of nowhere with a ghost around.

My friend in the front seat described him exactly as I had seen him; he looked like he was from another era. He was unusually tall, wearing overalls and a red shirt and had a tattered cowboy hat on. He was in the middle of my lane and my car passed right through him.

Abby, Chris, and their cousins loved this story.

Mom was up next and she told us about driving with her friend one night in Europe.

They were both tired and had been driving for many hours. They looked over to the car next to them and swore they saw a car full of pink bunnies.

The next time they went past the car, the bunnies were gone.

I'm not sure about ghost pink bunnies, but it got a laugh out of all of us, and I'm sure that was what she was going for anyway. The kids had loved my ghost story, but it made them a little afraid, so Grandma transformed the fear with something fun.

Then she talked about her friend Mark who had died a month before Mom had her surgery at MD Anderson. Mark and Mom were best friends. He lived in San Francisco and Mom would visit him often. When she arrived, he would pick her up in his yellow Mercedes, and they drove around town and around California in style, laughing and talking and causing trouble everywhere they went. Good trouble, but trouble nonetheless. Since Mark had died, Mom saw yellow cars as a sign that he was saying hello.

Just as she was telling the story, a yellow Mercedes drove by.

Jaden then talked about his grandfather. His grandfather had died of cancer when he was very young. Jaden was asleep in his bed, and he felt someone touch his foot. He opened his eyes and saw his grandfather. It made him both happy and sad all at the same time.

While we were telling all these stories, it came to me that the kids would remember telling stories like this with Mom. Having an open mind about life after death definitely helps all of us open our hearts to possibilities. What part of us dies? Of course our bodies die, but what about our spirit?

All of us considered this together in a lighthearted way on the drive to Madrid. It was a great way to think about life and death with the kids.

Chapter Twenty-One

Writing on the Soul

A little over a year before Mom died, she and I went to our favorite place in the world, Moab, Utah. In the last couple of years of Mom's life, her health was very fragile, and it was a bit of a risk to go out in the middle of nowhere with no hospitals nearby.

Mom's strong spirit was always apparent, but her body tired easily. She could get severely dehydrated quickly or she could get a mucous plug and not be able to breathe. She was on blood thinners for her cancer that could cause excessive bleeding, and she was highly susceptible to illness because her immune system was compromised from the chemo and radiation. It was incredibly helpful to be near a hospital.

It felt worth it to have an adventure, so we went to Moab anyway.

We stopped overnight in Durango, Colorado, and explored their main street, shopping and eating along the way. We went to the old Strater Hotel and listened to live music and had drinks and dinner. Even with Mom's fragile health, she brightened the room, mouthing the words to the songs and talking with her talker and making everyone around her smile.

It was always such a mixed bag of reactions to Mom when we went out together. Some people were respectful and would help me with Mom's walker and would really engage with her, and some people were bugged by the inconvenience of having to move and interact so gently. Her frail body took consciousness to be around, and she could be knocked over or harmed really easily.

That night, the hotel bar was a tight squeeze, and everyone was kind and friendly and helpful. Getting Mom to the bathroom was quite a navigational puzzle because it was a long way down a flight of stairs and through a lobby. Somehow we managed it, but it was not an easy task.

Bumping along through the bar, the music loud in our ears, Mom held on to me with a feeling of safety and comfort. She knew I had her. I knew she had me. We were a good team.

With all the health issues Mom had, a lot of thought had to be taken for every choice we made. Was the place wheelchair or walker accessible? If not, how would she maneuver? Did she need a wheelchair, a cane, a walker, a scooter, or a combination? Where could I park? Was there a place to drop Mom off? How could I keep Mom safe if there was a crowd? Did she have her talker? Had she charged the battery on her talker? Did she have enough batteries for her talker so they would last the day? Did she have her trach care kit? So many questions came into play on the simplest decisions in a day.

We had to be really present and grounded in every action. This was not a natural state for Mom or for me. We tended to be people who flew by the seat of our pants in most areas of our lives. While we couldn't be that way anymore, the consciousness required for every choice made us grateful for everything we accomplished in a way that we had forgotten to be along our path in life.

After Durango, we headed to Moab, and my GPS took me a wild and weird way through Colorado. GPS is funny that way. It takes me on the least likely roads and makes me think that it's leading me down a path to be shot and killed by some GPS-generated person.

This time we were on a two-lane highway that went along a lake. It was beautiful, pristine, and blue.

Every time I was with Mom near water, I would have a strange feeling of vertigo. If she fell into the water, she would drown because she breathed out of a hole in her neck, and she couldn't cover it to hold her breath.

Unfortunately, Mom's chemo brain had made her less likely to be careful around water. I carried the weight of remembering things for her a lot, and her breathing and lack of being able to breathe under water was one of them.

I've had vertigo throughout my life, and it's a feeling of being drawn to something dangerous, like a cliff or a lake right next to the road. Needless to say, we made it past the beautiful lake without drowning, and the GPS got us to familiar roads and the path to Moab.

Moab is the land of red rock, arches, and striking blue skies. It is a bit like landing on Mars, except it's a friendly environment with smiling people, good food, and breathtaking landscapes. There were no aliens, except maybe Mom with her pink hair, walker, and robot voice, and me, her trusty sidekick.

We had my dogs with us so we went searching for arches outside of Arches National Park. There are no dogs allowed in the National Parks, and I wanted to be able to walk with them.

We bought a map of all the arches and petroglyphs in the area, and we picked the road to the Jug Handle Arch. When we turned at the sign, we looked around and didn't see the arch, so we started down a rutted dirt road in my four-wheel drive.

We kept driving.

We kept driving.

We kept driving, bumping along this dirt road, and I suddenly wondered, what if we got stuck?

Here I was with my fragile mom in the middle of nowhere, with no cell phone service, down a dirt road alone.

Mom was scared of four-wheel drive in general and this road was pretty rutted. She began to verbalize her anxiety.

It gave us both pause and we faced the precariousness of life together. There was sweetness in the fact that we were in it together, and there was fear that we both faced in constant ways.

My fear was whether I could take care of Mom to the best of my abilities, both in terms of her health and in terms of her mental, emotional, and spiritual well-being.

Her fears were around dying, living well, and suffering mentally, emotionally, physically, and spiritually.

The sweetness was the bond between Mom and I that had always been apparent in our life together, but that had deepened in her dying process.

We sat with the sweetness and the fear and then we turned around.

Of course, we got out alive, and when we got to the main road, we looked up and there was the Jug Handle Arch. Right by the road! How we had missed it is anyone's guess, but the journey on the dirt road was worth it. We had faced our fears, we sat with the sweetness, and we could tackle the next challenge.

On the way back from the Jug Handle Arch we searched for the petroglyphs that were shown on our map. There were a bunch of them along the road.

Mom loved seeing the ancient writing and storytelling that the petroglyphs portrayed. As an English teacher, her inclination for storytelling and art was always on the surface ready to be discussed and investigated.

There were rock walls covered with symbolic carvings representing fertility, hunting, spirituality, animals, and families. We talked about the various images, what they might have represented, and what they meant to us.

It did our hearts good to see history written on the rocks. In a way, that is Mom's history with me now. While there is nothing as visible drawn on me as the petroglyphs, her story in my heart feels as clear as the writing on the rocks.

We couldn't find one particular petroglyph of a bear that felt important to us to find. Mom and I saw bears as a symbol of strength. We both needed to connect with our inner strength often on our journey together, so finding the bear felt like it would bring us extra energy for the days to come.

Finally, we saw it, large and somewhat isolated from the other petroglyphs. I climbed up to it and Mom stayed near the car. I called down to her; she looked up and we had a moment of connection that sticks with me in my memory. It brought me back to childhood when she would patiently wait while I climbed a tree or did a tightrope walk along a curb.

My mom, holding space for me to be me. She held that space throughout my life until the very end.

Every morning in Moab we would go to the same restaurant and have crepes and coffee. Watching Mom find pleasure in food and drink was one of my favorite things. Everything was *soooo* good, *soooo* satisfying. At breakfast, we would contemplate our escapades and daydream about the day to come. The days were always brighter and better than we could dream up in our heads.

We went to Arches National Park before we left. There were signs there for bighorn sheep, and we always scoured the hillsides to see if we could spot one, but we never did.

While at the park, we ate lunch in a shaded picnic area surrounded by red rock. Then Mom and the dogs took a nap in the car and I hiked. There was a powerful wind that day that blew people's hats off and stirred the sand to make cloud-like patterns along the ground. I could visualize the sandstone reshaping into new landscapes with that powerful wind. On that day, we were a part of future history, our time together carving into the stone.

Chapter Twenty-Two

Navigating the Storm

A friend asked me how I was able to be healthy in my life while also dealing with Mom's illness.

At the time she asked, we had just gone through another of the many visits to the hospital, and I had to cancel all of my clients and rearrange everything in order to deal with the need to be there for Mom. Balancing helping Mom with my work and my life was vital, but it wasn't an easy task. Taking care of her was a full-time job with an unpredictable schedule that often meant a lot of overtime.

There was a need for intense focus in order to not feel crushed by all of the daily chores for Mom's care. It was exhausting to deal with the ever-evolving news, the emotions that would rise up, and the constant trauma.

There were multiple times when I got into the car and let go of a stream of swear words or a had good cry. I would definitely say that swearing and crying helped me release a buildup of emotions and were lifesavers at times.

I also had to learn to stay present in the moment. I had known that the present moment was all there was, and ultimately there was no past, no future, only now. I understood the concept of this in my mind before this time of my life, but I had never fully had to practice it in the way that I did with Mom's illness.

I needed to be impeccably conscious of my thoughts. When they started to run in circles about the trials and tribulations we were facing without finding any solutions, I would ask my thoughts to stop. I asked my mind to be present.

When a lot of crises were happening and my mind would feel overwhelmed and ready to collapse, I would really have to bring my thoughts to a stopping point by saying something like this to myself: "Be here now, be present, be in this moment. Solve what can be solved now and let go of the rest. Be patient with the unfolding. Let go of what cannot be controlled. Be here now."

It's interesting, because the doctors always said, "Control what you can and let go of the rest." That is a great concept but not an easy practice.

I learned to let go of worry. I am saying I *let go of worry,* but I am not saying that I did not worry. Fear is a part of our survival mind. It alerts us to danger and helps us to perceive threats in our lives. Worry comes from fear. I needed to witness the worry and see if there was anything I could do to assuage it. If there was nothing I could do with it, then I would consciously let it go. This is much easier said than done, but it was a vital part of my practice so I could stay centered.

My investigation when it came to worry went something like this: I would ask myself, "Is there anything I can do today to work with what I'm worrying about?"

If the answer was yes, I would take care of what I could right then. For example, I may have worried that I needed to pay my bills. I realized I could sit and write the checks to pay my bills and the worry was gone.

If the answer was no, I asked for healing energy to embrace my heart and support me in letting go of the fear that was underlying the worry. For example, I would worry that Mom was suffering and experiencing emotional, mental, physical, or spiritual pain. In this case, the worry was out of my control. I could talk her through things and send her light and healing, but most of what she needed to go through with cancer was a part of her path, and nothing I could fix.

It was a lot more difficult to let go of the esoteric worry, and it required a huge amount of talking through in my heart and mind.

From conversations with Mom, I know she struggled most with the esoteric worry as well. The fear of death is the ultimate existential fear. What comes next? Will I be okay? Will everyone I love be okay? All of those questions woke her up at night and gripped her.

When we went to the doctor, her biggest complaint was always anxiety. There was no good solution for her because she couldn't talk with counselors, and she did not want to be overly medicated.

Her doctor gave her a prescription for medical marijuana. Because she could not smoke it with her trach she was limited in options, but she got a tincture that took away some of the gripping worries in the night. It saved Mom's sanity and allowed her to sleep when nothing else could.

When distressing news about her health or treatment came up, both Mom and I struggled with multiple floods of emotions.

I felt the emotions as they came. If I was sad, I felt sad. If I was angry, I felt angry. If I was happy, I felt happy. I tried not to take the emotions out on others; I just let myself feel them. This allowed me to move with the flow of what was going on with Mom and with myself. It helped me stay present and allowed me to appreciate the times that were calm without having background noise in my heart and mind.

Mom had more difficulty dealing with emotions. Because she wasn't able to express them out loud she felt trapped by them sometimes. With her talker she could talk to me, she could talk to Mike, she could talk to Aunt Betty, and she could talk with a couple of friends, but she struggled with processing all that she needed to process out loud. She couldn't articulate everything as extensively as she was used to.

Mom and I learned to discuss challenging things more thoroughly than we ever had before. Because Mom was so sick and could be severely incapacitated, there was no way to avoid important topics. I was her medical power of attorney and needed to know what she would want if she was unable to decide for herself, and I also wanted to know her as completely as I could before I lost her.

By not shying away from conversations about life and death and everywhere in between, Mom and I became closer than we had ever been. We knew when to get real with each other, and we also knew how to have silly, meaningless conversations when we needed a break from the intensity of all that was happening.

I would say Mom's and my greatest strength in this journey together was to remember to find things that brought us joy every day. No matter what was going on in life, finding joy was vital. Some days it was easy to see and find. On the harder days, the small things got us through. We would find joy in a beautiful sky, a bird's song, a dog's wagging tail, or a friend's voice.

I remember one particularly intense visit to the emergency room. There was a man withdrawing from drugs, writhing on the ground and moaning on the floor next to us, and a woman in a wheelchair screaming and groaning loudly about her pain off and on. No one was helping any of us, and it was incredibly tough not to get lost in the despair. I brought out my phone and Mom, our friend Loyce, and I watched videos of birds that I had taken. We watched them over and over for eight hours until they finally took care of Mom and she was released.

I am empathic and I feel energy and my surroundings intensely. Going to hospitals where people were dealing with trauma and illness had never been an easy thing for me. Since we went to the hospital often, I practiced turning my focus from the heaviness I saw and connecting with beauty and love instead. Centering my attention on something inspiring like the bird videos or on a loving act I would witness lifted my spirit and fueled me. Nurses or aides being kind to patients always filled my heart, and someone who was kind to Mom or me was extra meaningful. I would consciously expand the feeling those experiences would bring to my heart, and I could feel the love inside myself strengthen.

When situations or energy would start to affect me negatively, I would return to the beauty I saw. That turn of focus would allow me to make it through our visits to the hospitals with some level of grace.

Mom and I also practiced gratitude, kindness, and love. We could focus on the love we saw and also share that love with others by embodying it. We would ask people about their lives and listen to them. We would look people in the eyes and thank them. We would do anything we could to expand the goodness around us.

When tough times came into our lives, we learned to embrace them.

For me, when I felt resistance to experiencing something in my body, mind, heart, or soul, I investigated the resistance and prayed for help in letting go of whatever was creating it. Bracing against or avoiding issues just made them worse.

I have artwork in my house that says, "The obstacle is the path." This is something I practiced daily. Instead of avoiding the obstacles, I learned to walk through them. Sometimes they were little hills like having to make a phone call I didn't want to make, and sometimes they were Mt. Everests, like going to Mom's deathbed to say goodbye. Each obstacle, big or small, was necessary for me to face.

When I let go of the need to brace myself against a problem, I was able to investigate it, allow it into my life, learn from it, and let it move through my life.

The biggest hurdle for me was letting myself be human and letting myself completely fail at self-care and care for Mom at times. As much as I knew there was a bigger picture and a beauty in the madness, there were times when I could only see the drama before me, and it felt so large that I became paralyzed. Because I had my tools, I got through the paralysis, but I'm only human after all.

The places where I failed the most were in the practical realm.

There were many times my house looked like a hurricane had gone through it because I didn't have the time or energy to clean.

There were many times when I couldn't figure out what to eat and would get takeout.

Taking care of the mundane parts of life was hard for me, and I failed and fell behind often, but the worst part was when I was short with Mom or short with myself because I was tired.

One day she texted me, "I lost my talker."

Mom was always losing her talker, her cell phone, and her purse. She couldn't keep track of things.

"You don't know where you had it last?" I texted.

"No. I am freaking out. I can't find it anywhere."

It was about 10:00 p.m. and I was tired.

"Could we wait until the morning and I will come and help you find it?" I texted.

"No, I need it now. What if there's an emergency and I can't talk?"

"But you're just going to be asleep."

"I need it NOW."

I went over and she was in a full-blown panic attack. We scoured her whole apartment, and finally she realized she must have left it in the game room where she had played cards that night. The game room was locked and we couldn't get in until the morning.

I sat with her late into the night until she finally fell asleep and I returned first thing in the morning. Her talker wasn't in the game room, and Mom went into full despair thinking she could not talk. These machines were $800 and we could not just go to a store to buy one, so losing it was not an option. It turned out that one of her friends had taken it home with her and didn't understand that it would stress Mom out not to have it.

I was exhausted and impatient and tired by the end of the saga and was short with her when I left.

The greatest gift was that Mom always loved me anyway, and I always loved her.

We talked later that day, and she expressed that she understood I was exhausted and frustrated. I told her I understood her panic attack and fear.

Finding unconditional love with someone you've known for over forty years is a miracle and so rare. It got us through the hardest phase of our lives with grace.

Chapter Twenty-Three

Jesus in the Grocery Store

As Mom's cancer progressed, she continued to wake up to living. It opened her heart, and she began to smile with her whole being as well as her body. I saw her embark on all types of friendships she might not have made in the past. She was open in a way she hadn't been for as long as I could remember.

Mom didn't follow a specific religion, but if I was to give her a religion that was close to what she was, it would be Buddhism. At her independent living home, she became best friends with a Born-Again Christian.

Mom would call me and say, "Shirley prayed to Jesus for me at lunch."

"Did you like it?" I asked.

"Yes, it was sweet," she would say.

Mom had become accepting where she might have been shut down in her former life, and her heart was softer and more tolerant.

This allowed her mind to relax around different beliefs that in her past would have held her back from an experience.

She and Shirley were like sisters at heart, and Mom even went to church with Shirley and her family a couple of Sundays. It started to seem like the family was trying to save her soul, and Mom was comfortable with her soul and her beliefs. She stopped attending church with them, but she stopped without drama and without blame. I remember having long discussions with her about how to tell them she didn't want to go anymore. She didn't want to hurt their feelings, and she just wanted them to feel her gratitude.

She was able to communicate it well, and she and Shirley remained fast friends until Shirley moved to another state.

A lot of people would come up to Mom and pray over her wherever we went. Strangers would see Mom looking frail and want to help her. Sometimes their way of helping was to pray.

It was always a bit of a shock, because Mom and I got so used to her circumstances that we forgot her illness was visible with her walker, her talker, and her trach. We also got so caught up in the fun of life that we almost forgot about her cancer.

Strangers would come up to us and say, "Can I pray for you?" Mom would always say yes, and then the person would start a loud prayer to Jesus over Mom wherever we were. It seemed to come from such a pure and loving place from the people who did it, but it was always just a little odd. Imagine being in the grocery checkout line with someone praying loudly for Jesus to heal you. Definitely not an ordinary moment.

Those extra-ordinary—and I am spelling that intentionally—those moments that were more than ordinary, happened so often with Mom that the miraculous became normal. Without those miracles,

Mom and I might have forgotten the higher perspective along the way. Cancer brought so many less-than-pretty physical realities, that we had to look to the spirit in life and stay focused on that in order to thrive.

Toward the very end of Mom's life, she had some angels in human form come to her and pray and sing and love on her.

At one point, Mom had fallen and injured herself. We had gotten her home healthcare, and I had the camera in her room so I could see what was going on and check on her.

The first day, I checked to make sure the home healthcare person had arrived, and I saw this strong muscular middle-aged man in scrubs come into the room and immediately start singing to her. "Hey, hey good looking, what you got cooking, how about cooking something up for me?" I could hear Mom laugh, "beep beep beep," and knew she was in good hands. He was gentle and loving with her and prayed and sang to her as he got her up and dressed. Mom later told me he sang to her in Spanish, Italian, German, and Chinese! She loved it.

I never met that particular angel, but every morning I checked on her, he was there with a big smile making Mom laugh.

When Mom was being transferred to her final home, one of the men who helped with the transfer was a very kind Christian who asked if he could pray for her. He did so very loudly when we answered yes.

Mom was in another land in her mind at that point and had a dreamy look on her face when they wheeled her to the ambulance. The medical transport driver sang hymns all the way.

The man fell in love with Mom, gave me a big hug when we met at her facility, and said Mom was an angel. That was very true, and he was an angel as well.

In embracing life and love and relationship at the end of her life, Mom made up for lost time. She may have forgotten at some points in her journey that engaging with people could awaken gratitude in her and could awaken it in others as well, but she remembered it fully at the end of her life. Her life and mine were filled with miracles because of it.

Chapter Twenty-Four

Doing Pretty Good

As I am writing this, I am approaching Mom's birthday. She was born on the third of July after 11:00 p.m., and her dad always called her "almost a firecracker." Mom definitely lived up to that name since she always enlivened a room just like fireworks fill the sky with light, energy, and sound.

While I was driving to my office to write this, I thought of Mom and of her last birthday. She was really beginning to fail at that point. Her chemotherapy was starting to fight her back.

I remember going to dinner a couple of months before her birthday; we were driving home.

"I think I am going to throw up," Mom said.

I looked over at her and she looked a little green.

"Are you going to throw up right now?" I asked and she nodded.

I tried to pull over, but didn't make it in time, and she got sick all over the car and then again all over the street.

Mom was incredibly inspiring while she was living, but I don't want to create any illusions about the dying process. Watching the physical body dying can be a terrible thing. Especially when a person is like Mom who wanted to squeeze every drop out of life. She didn't take to her bed because of cancer, she got out in the world to see people and explore. None of what she went through was behind closed doors.

There was so much beauty we experienced while she was sick, and there were many gross, uncomfortable, scary, emotionally devastating, and just plain hard circumstances as well. The beauty outweighed the tough stuff in my memories, but the tough stuff was there. It was challenging to be Mom, and it was challenging to be one of the people who loved her. Finding the silver lining and the goodness in her path took all of our emotional, mental, physical, and spiritual strength at times.

After Mom threw up, I drove her home and walked her to her room. She said she felt better, and I helped her get ready for bed and went home. It was late and I spent the night cleaning out the car.

Our solution to this new development was to carry a plastic bag around in case she needed to get sick.

What I loved about Mom in many of these circumstances was that it never occurred to her to give up or give in. It never crossed her mind that if she might spontaneously throw up, she should stay home.

We had some gross moments along the way, but they lasted only a moment, and then we did our best to move on.

On Mom's last birthday, her seventy-eighth, we went up to Santa Fe. It's interesting as I sit here and think back to her birthday; I have no recollection of what we did that day.

In the last few months of her life everything was meaningful, but there was also a lot of trauma, and it seems that the trauma erased some of my memories.

She went to the hospital for dehydration on multiple occasions. As much as we could do to keep her hydrated, her body just couldn't get the fluids it needed, and her mind struggled with remembering to drink. It certainly didn't help that she lived in the hot and dry desert.

There was a knowing that death was near.

I think back to the doctor's appointments, and I remember that her cancer numbers were starting to climb again. She was needing more chemo, but she was also showing signs of rejecting the chemo.

Even when I write this, I start to get agitated and look for something else to do other than write about this time.

How was I feeling? I wanted to be upbeat, but I was exhausted. This was the fifth year of Mom's cancer treatment. Every month, there was a new development that required more care on my part.

It was as if I was approaching the final mile of a marathon and I realized that the last mile was all uphill and I had to sprint.

Could I really do it?

I can imagine Mom feeling her body start to shut down. As much as she had fought the cancer, her body couldn't live forever.

One day, my phone started getting text after text during a session with a client. I lost focus and had to reschedule. One of my friends was with Mom, and she had started slurring her words and speaking gibberish. I told her to call the paramedics and met Mom at the hospital. She couldn't sit still and was inconsolably agitated. She was most likely in a full-blown panic attack, but she had arrived at the hospital without her talker and therefore without the ability to speak.

While this was happening, a respiratory therapist came in to clean her trach. He was obnoxiously joking around and teasing Mom while poking and prodding at her. Most of the times when we went to the hospital, the people who cared for her were awesome, but this guy was clueless.

I kept telling him that Mom needed anxiety medicine and that she needed him to come back later. He just completely ignored me and kept poking at her, wanting to learn about her larytube because it was like nothing he had ever seen before.

I finally got rid of him and Mom's whole body shook from the stress and anxiety.

When Mom had these panic attacks mixed with dehydration, it really appeared like she was dying. Her skin color went gray, her mind was not clear, and she was unable to be comforted or diverted from her anxiety. It was a terrible thing for her to experience, and it was a terrible thing to witness.

They gave her fluids and anxiety medicine, and she was sent home late that evening.

I think Mom held so much stress about dying that occasionally it just took over and her whole body shut down. She got through it and then was good for a while, but I know she felt underlying angst a lot along the way.

Mom didn't take her anxiety or her stress out on me or anyone else. She had every reason to turn into an angry person, but she didn't.

Most times when I would go see Mom, even at the hardest times, I would ask how she was doing and she would respond, "pretty good." I can still hear her voice in the midst of trauma. "I'm doing pretty good."

If she can be pretty good in the midst of all she was going through, then nothing in life is ultimately worth worrying about.

Chapter Twenty-Five

Dying Well

"Be at peace with my passing."

These are the words I feel and hear when I sit down to write today. I have been able to see, hear, feel, and know the voice of the divine throughout my life. I sit some more to see if anything else comes to me, but that is it for the day. I guess that says it all, really.

I have learned over the years that the divine voice speaks simply, without embellishments. That is very different from Mom's personality here on earth. Everything was embellished. She spoke loudly, she was not shy, and she charged into situations with vitality and spunk.

This served her well when she got cancer. No part of her wanted to lie down and die. She was ready to conquer cancer and live.

The interesting thing that everyone knows, of course, is that we are all going to die. No matter how much we might want to live, death comes for every single human being.

After the trip to the hospital where Mom had such an intense panic attack, I called my brother and asked him to come be with Mom. It was never certain which life-threatening ailment would be her last. She had some pretty dramatic moments with her health that most people would not have made it through, and it was always complicated to gauge when to tell people to come.

Since Mom recovered from her hospital visit and was "doing pretty good," the three of us decided to go to Moab together, and Aunt Betty and Uncle Tibor met us there.

It was significant for all of us to get to be at Mom's most treasured travel destination with her. Mike had never been to Moab and we had a lot to show him. He and I hiked for hours looking at arches and petroglyphs while Mom and Aunt Betty talked and giggled about life together. Their bond was fun to witness. They were sisters, but not just by birth. They were soul sisters as well.

Aunt Betty and Mom had been born eighteen months apart. Mom was a brunette and Aunt Betty was a blonde, but when they got older and their hair turned gray, they looked like twins. Throughout their lives, they talked with each other often. When Mom got sick, Aunt Betty sent cards regularly, helped research and set up care for her, visited frequently, and talked with her on Skype at least once a week if not more. The support they gave to each other was unshakable, and their connection never wavered.

While we were in Moab, the sacredness of a lifelong relationship that only siblings have was present—Mom with Aunt Betty and me with Mike. Uncle Tibor grounded us and gave us all the space we needed to connect.

There was a day when we all went to the Arches National Park. Mom was sitting on her wheelchair with an umbrella to block the sun, and we all walked closer to one of the arches than Mom was able to go to on the gravel trail. I turned around and saw a couple of men carrying her wheelchair to get her near the arch. She was not satisfied with her view so she got help to fix that problem.

We were the ones who carried her back, and she was heavy!

On our final night together, we made reservations at a nice restaurant to celebrate our trip, and we were all filled with high spirits as we drove there. When we sat down, we were laughing and telling stories. Mom wanted to drink whiskey and eat trout to honor my grandpa and grandma, but she suddenly looked a bit green. In our reverie, we had all forgotten for a moment the severity of her illness. It was instantly apparent.

The bathroom was down some stairs that Mom couldn't navigate on her own. An incredible waitress offered to help. She lifted my mom gently, and carried her down the long staircase so Mom could be sick.

On the way home from the restaurant, there was silence in the car. It was a somber moment; the highs and lows in this journey were extreme, and they gave us emotional whiplash at times.

We were glad to have seized the moment to gather together.

When our visit was over, Mike caught a bus north to the airport in Salt Lake City. A young woman in her twenties hopped on the bus with her dog last minute. She looked like Mom when she was young, and she had the same feeling of freedom that Mom had embodied throughout her life. Mike and I looked at each other for a moment and smiled a happy and sad smile as the bus took off to the north carrying them both away.

Mom and I drove south to Albuquerque. She and I talked the whole way home about her dying. The drive is about eight hours, so this was a long discussion.

I wish I had a recording of the conversation because it was sweet and innocent and also rich and meaningful, but there were a few things that really stood out in my memory.

She expressed that she felt like no one really wanted to talk with her about her struggles with her disease and her dying.

This was interesting because Mom rarely gave an opening to talk about death. There has to be a willingness on both sides to have the tough conversations. I tended to push through with her and kept asking questions so that she had to talk about what was going on for her. Without that persistence, we might not have discussed death like we did. In her mind, though, it was resistance on other people's part to talk about what was really going on.

She said people wanted her to be positive and not negative. Talking about death, she continued, meant giving up and they wouldn't talk to her about it. This may have been her own perception that she projected onto other people.

I wish I had Mom's voice to share here about this topic, but I couldn't find anything she wrote about it.

Death is not positive or negative; it is just a part of reality. It never felt like Mom and I were being negative by discussing the reality that she would die from this cancer.

Encouraging her to tackle the cancer to the best of her body's ability was fitting. That was clearly what she wanted to do. She desired to live as well as she could for as long as she could and was very vocal about that.

Discussing the fact that her life would end also made sense because that was the reality of what she was going through. She talked about the anxiety that she felt often. She was less able to be mobile, and she sat with the weight of dying a lot. Talking about it took some of that weight away, she said.

The only way to get Mom into a conversation about death was to push. I had to be stubborn about asking, otherwise she would deflect the conversation or just flat out say she didn't want to talk about it.

We explored all of this as we drove through the beautiful desert landscapes of Utah, Colorado, and New Mexico.

We had processed a lot about what we were afraid of with death and the dying process, so I asked Mom if there was anything that she looked forward to in death, for instance meeting people and animals who had died, since both Mom and I believed in life after death.

She liked the idea of looking forward to something on the other side.

Her immediate first answer was her dog Rosie and her best friend Mark, and then she contemplated other friends and family who had died.

Mom loved the thought of seeing her dad, but then she paused.

"I'm scared to see my mom," she said.

I asked her why and she said, "I don't know that my mom and I ever understood each other. I never really forgave her for being different from me and for being so hard on me. I think I was equally hard on her."

She sat with that thought in silence for a little while and then said, "My pastime as a child was collecting and playing with paper dolls. I loved everything about it and spent hours playing pretend situations with them. I loved fashion from a very young age and began to design and draw clothes for the dolls that I had.

"Then on Sundays, I would look through the ads for department stores like Chapmans and Boston Store, and I would copy the hand drawings of the new dresses. They often had drawings then instead of pictures.

"I kept my paper dolls in a shoebox in my closet, and one day my mom threw them out in a cleaning frenzy. I was heartbroken. I felt as if I had lost my best friends."

Mom spent her life repairing her relationship with her mom in her heart and mind. My grandmother, whose name was Rose, died when I was in high school and when Mom was fifty. When Mom moved to New Mexico, she found a beautiful black husky dog and named her Rosie so she could heal the relationship with her mom by experiencing unconditional love for and from her dog. Mom loved Rosie the most out of all of the dogs she ever had.

While we talked on the drive about Grandma Rose, Mom processed more disappointment in herself than anger at her mom. She wished she had been more understanding of Grandma and more willing to see her point of view.

It was a fascinating conversation for me, and one that we had never had.

I had not realized Mom would be scared to see Grandma, and it was intriguing to me that it would cause resistance to dying. I encouraged Mom to talk to Grandma in her heart and work on what she might want to say to her.

"Mom, I love you and I'm sorry," was the essence of what she wanted to say, and I told her to keep connecting with Grandma so they could heal.

We watched the landscape go by and enjoyed the thought of forgiveness.

The last thing that stood out in our conversation about death was that Mom was afraid of not "dying well." I asked her what she meant by that.

She knew she was stubbornly holding on to life. She was conscious about wanting to squeeze every bit of life she could out of the experience she was having as Diana Bee Steffen. She feared that when the time came she wouldn't be able to let go and actually die. I told her that no matter how much she resisted, eventually her body would die. She couldn't hold it off forever. Death was a natural process, and no matter how much she tried to hold on, she would eventually let go.

We laughed about the thought of dying well. I told her no one would judge her if she couldn't let go for a while. She wasn't going to get a prize if she died well. She wasn't going to get a black mark against her soul if she died poorly. It would be okay.

This thought of dying well came up quite a bit during Mom's journey toward dying. She very clearly had a hard time letting go of life because she very clearly *loved* this life. Over her last five years, she might have died many times.

This was Mom's path and she did it her way. She kept bouncing back, and every time she bounced back we would have great experiences and significant conversations. One thing was clear: This was *her* journey, her life, and her choice.

As I was contemplating writing this chapter, I realized that some part of me was experiencing something similar to Mom. I don't know if I am grieving well or correctly. This thought surprised me, because I am not one to consciously question my journey.

I know that grief, like dying, is individual to each person. It will take as long as it takes. Each stage will heal when it needs to heal.

One thing I love feeling as the days unfold and I heal more and more from my grief is the inspiration from Mom when it comes to living. The "I love life!" declaration she made at the end of her life echoes in my heart and teaches me to live.

She may have stubbornly held on to life. She may have created some suffering for herself and others along the way, but through it all, she lived. Brightly, with spirit and style. She lived.

Chapter Twenty-Six

People Say Awkward Things

The rich conversations that Mom and I had about life and death were profound and transformational for me.

They bring to mind a challenge I encountered. Talking to other people about what I was going through was often awkward. We live in a culture that doesn't know how to talk about hardships and death.

My conversations with other people about Mom's situation could be much more taxing than talking to her in a real way about what she was facing.

The most common thing that many people told me was that they would never do what she was doing—they would just want to let go and die. They would say this to me casually as though it was not a shocking thing to say.

It always made me feel awkward, and I would say something like, "Well, I'm glad she's still here." Or, I would just change the subject.

What someone else would do in Mom's circumstance was theoretical and did not really have relevance.

It was supportive when people took the "I" out of the conversation. Some people asked me, "How are you feeling with all that is going on?" Or they stated, "Your mom is inspiring with her will to live," and these words comforted me.

Another awkward thing people would say was that they would never put me through what my mother was putting me through by "making" me care for her.

This comment always startled me and made me pause.

I consciously decided to care for Mom. There weren't a lot of other options for support. Her disabilities and her disease made it difficult to find other help, but being able to be there for Mom was profound for me.

It helped me when people asked, "How are you feeling taking care of your mom?" Or, when they said, "I respect what you are doing for your mom."

No one knows what they would do with cancer unless they actually have it. No one knows what they would do when someone close to them has cancer. Being empathetic requires inquiring and listening and being present. When people gave me room to tell them what I was experiencing, I felt supported and heard.

Mom had such an incredible love for life and a gratitude for the world around her. Getting to be with her through her dying process was one of the most positive things I have ever experienced. Positive didn't mean happy all the time; it meant being real and awake for all that came my way, and from that place I was able to grow.

When people were present with love, I could feel it. It made off-putting things that they said okay in the end. I understood that no one knew what to say. I've been in similar situations, and I am certain that I have spoken words that were hard for people to hear.

I learned from all of my experiences to be inquisitive and to meet people where they are at in all situations, especially in conversations about death and dying.

Chapter Twenty-Seven

The Land of the In-Between

Toward the end of Mom's life, in the fall of 2017, she had a serious reaction to her chemotherapy, became severely dehydrated, and had to go to the emergency room. Every time we went it was a bit scary, but this was a new level of reaction; it turned out her body was no longer tolerating the chemo.

Usually, when she went to the hospital she was just there for a few hours or overnight. On this occasion, she was admitted, given a room, and stayed for over a week.

While we were there, she was extremely disoriented. I caught a glimpse of what it might be like to have a parent with Alzheimer's, and it gave me even more compassion than I already had for those who have dealt with the disease. Mom always knew who I was, but often couldn't figure out where she was. She was weak in her body and in her mind.

When she started to be able to move around a little, I would hold her arm and walk her through the halls of the hospital. We created a fantasy world. Since Mom didn't know where she was, I asked her where she would like to be. We would walk the streets of Manhattan or Paris together, and she would tell me what she loved about the cities.

Mom lived in Manhattan for a couple of years in her early twenties and always spoke of it fondly, so the streets would come alive in my mind as she described her explorations of the city. She would recount her favorite art at the Guggenheim, the MOMA, and the Metropolitan Museum of Art; talk through the great food that she ate at restaurants, and speak of the diversity of the cultures and people that she encountered along the way. We would visit her friends Susan and Marsha and walk through Washington Square and Greenwich Village in our minds.

In Paris, we would imagine ourselves visiting Notre Dame and lighting candles for the people we loved. Walking along the Seine, we visited street vendors, looked at art and old books, and spoke French badly. When we reached the Eiffel Tower, we would sit at a cafe and drink espresso and wine and eat steak au poivre avec pommes frites and creme brulee.

In real life, we were traipsing slowly down a hospital hall with nurses and aides and patients all around us.

When we reached the end of the hallway, we would look out the window and watch people and cars go by, and we daydreamed about all that we enjoyed about life.

Mom would talk about having pints with her friends Kevin and Phil on the Memorial Union Terrace in Madison, Wisconsin, and tell stories about the mischief they would get up to. She daydreamed about laughing with them again.

We could see a busy street from the window, and we looked for yellow cars and signs that Mark was with us. We laughed because a lot of nurses had yellow pants and we thought it was a creative way for Mark to say hello. Yellow cars, yellow pants. Same difference. It was a very special time.

Mom's good friend Loyce shared with me that one of her favorite moments with Mom before she died was when she visited the hospital during this period. Mom started telling her all about her life in New York. She was a successful writer and a book editor. She went to the theater, saw the ballet, and hung out with friends every night. At first Loyce was startled and wondered if Mom was describing an era in her life that Loyce did not know about. Then, she realized that she was in a fantasy world, and she had a great conversation exploring Mom's make-believe land with her.

I didn't expect to have Mom's mind come back. It seemed like she had entered an alternate universe; and while we daydreamed and had sweet times together, it also caused her anxiety when she would get pulled back into the world. Figuring out something simple like how to make a phone call would cause her severe panic attacks.

One of the things I learned in Mom's journey was to expect the unexpected.

After a week in the hospital, Mike and his family came to see her.

In the midst of her wandering mind, Chris and Abby came and brought her back. For Mom, being a mother was her favorite role, but being a grandmother was even more spectacular. In movies, there are films that are just in color and those that are in technicolor where the color pops and is amplified. Being a grandmother for Mom was like being a parent in technicolor. Her grandkids were her favorite things.

When she saw them, a spark came back in her eyes, and she became less inclined to wander off into fantasy land. Chris and Abby were Mom's superheroes. Their cape was woven from the love they all shared.

Mom was transferred to a nursing facility and given rehab. She expressed the desire to live, so we created the space for her to try.

While she was in the facility, Mom was starting to return to the world but she was still in an alternate reality. Because people could not understand what she was saying, they assumed she was better since she was walking and talking. She appeared fine, even though her mind was still very fuzzy.

There were times Mom fell deeply asleep for hours. Mike, Kim, Chris, Abby, and I went on a walk along the river during one of those times. While we were there, we played with the dogs in the water and I took a lot of photos.

We got back to Mom just as she woke up from her slumber. While we were there, she called Aunt Betty and started talking about how we all went to the river. She included herself as though she was there.

"We went down to the river and it was so FUN!" she said to my aunt. "It was beautiful out and we played in the water and played with the dogs! It was a great day!"

We all looked at each other because the way she described it made it seem like she had been there with us, even though she had been napping in her bed.

That night as I looked at the photos from the day, I saw that there was a kaleidoscope of light in a couple of pictures of the kids in the river that looked like an energy or a spirit. It was in the shape of a human figure that was illuminated by a rainbow running through it. In one photo it was right next to Chris and in the other it was right next to Abby.

I showed it to my family and we believed that Mom had actually been with us in some divine way, and we had photos to prove it.

A day or two later, Mike and everyone left and Mom started to lift out of her fog.

She and I went for a little walk. While we were walking, I realized that she was more conscious and aware. It was a shock. It was a good shock, but I had not expected her to come back and be coherent in her mind. I asked her if she remembered much from the last month. She said no, that it was kind of like remembering a dream. She remembered bits and pieces of it, but nothing concrete.

I asked her if she remembered being at the river, and she paused and stood still for a minute and said, "Yes, that I remember."

"Do you remember *being* there or hearing about it?" I asked.

"I remember *being* there," she said and paused. "I know I couldn't have been there, but I remember being there. I remember the kids playing with the dogs and a great feeling of joy."

"I feel like you were there, Mom," I said. "I feel like you experienced what death is. You will be with us. You will feel the joy with us. And if we are conscious of it, we can open our hearts to feel you with us as well."

Mom liked the thought. She struggled to grasp faith in an afterlife. She believed in life after death, but it was more of a concept in her mind than something she felt and experienced in her heart and in her full being.

When her mind left her and she was in an alternate reality, she started to have the *experience* of life after death. This helped her spirit and her soul find more peace. Life was not governed by her brain in those times, and she had to drop into another part of herself, an eternal part.

When she dropped into that eternal part, she found that some aspect of her, some essence, still existed, and that helped her prepare to let go.

She was released from rehab before she was ready to take care of herself. There are such amazing nurses and caregivers and administrators who truly care about their patients, and there are those who are focused on the bottom line of dollars and cents.

The rehab facility allowed Mom to sign her own release papers even though she wasn't mentally capable of doing so. They wouldn't answer my phone calls during the period of time where I could contest the decision, and I had to scramble to make sure she had the care she needed.

It took Mom another month to come back fully, but sure enough, we had her back for a couple more months. I didn't expect to be able to have clear conversations with her anymore, and it was such a gift.

Having had that "near-death" experience made Mom even more alert and aware that time was precious. She became even more present in the last couple of months of her life.

A few days after she was released from rehab, we walked to the river where we had gone with the family. It gave us both the chills to be able to walk the path together. She smiled, knowing that she had been there with the kids in spirit and was getting to be there with me now.

The fall leaves of the cottonwoods canopied us in vibrant yellow, and the river flowed by gently. A breeze moved through Mom's pink hair as we breathed in life together. The winds of change were upon us as she put her arm in mine and we stood with each other for a time enjoying the beauty.

Chapter Twenty-Eight

Rosie

Dreams about change (very rough).

I've never liked endings. I've tended to want things to last forever, clinging to the way things are and feeling sentimental about the past.

Now I've begun dreaming about endings. I had a long, vivid dream about a group of us moving out of a large warehouse space. It seemed we were in the movie business in some way, and the space was jam-packed with editing equipment. Wires were running everywhere.

I've done a fair amount of work as an extra in movies; New Mexico, with its sunny weather and financial support, had become a "new scene" in the movie business and extra work was fairly easy to come by, so movie sets were familiar to me.

It's not clear why we were moving out of this space, but what was certain was that we had to move out fast. We were working hard, hauling out large tables, and placing large pieces of equipment on dollies and putting them on U-Haul trucks.

A group of young whippersnappers was taking over the warehouse, and they were all standing around watching our move, anxious to move in. There was definitely a sense of the old moving out and the young moving in.

Suddenly I was at a meeting in a room next to the warehouse, and I could hear one woman from our group doing the final cleaning up of our space. I could hear her dragging some furniture out, the screeches echoing through space. I could hear her humming happily while she worked. I didn't feel guilty about not being there; I was just calmly listening to the work happening.

I got out of my meeting and came around the corner into the warehouse, and there it was in all of its grandeur.

Everything was completely cleaned out from one end to the other, and it was this beautiful empty space just waiting for something new. I was amazed to see the space completely cleaned out from one end to the other. It looked beautiful to me. There was a sense of openness and cleanliness. The space looked larger than before, and a sense of peace had settled in where there once was chaos.

There were a few things left hanging on the walls, and they reminded me of things my father had in his basement workspace in our house in Milwaukee so many years ago. A large landscape painting, a card with a statement about fishing with an oversized fishing hook attached, and a small picture of Jesus all hung in the warehouse. I wanted to take them with me, even made a move to take one of them off the wall, but resisted the urge and walked on out.

Suddenly, the youngsters had moved in. There was a tent up in one corner with the side flaps rolled up and a small group of them was gathered for a meeting. One guy was working at an editing machine, and two others were stacking things on a shelf that had been put up on one side.

Young whippersnappers, or were these people us? Had we become the young whippersnappers?

I felt no sadness about this move, just a quiet observation of all that was happening. This is not the way I would have felt about a move in the past in this life.

And now, of course, I'm faced on a daily basis with a change that I can't do anything about; Rosie passing away. Has this become the final piece in my process of accepting the flow of life, accepting change?

The dream brings to mind other endings in my life and my reactions to them.

Rosie's passing reminds me of my own mortality. The truth is that I don't wholly accept my own death. I just turned seventy this summer.

One of Mom's significant connections in her life was with her dog Rosie. They went everywhere together and they loved each other unequivocally. Two years after Rosie died, Mom got diagnosed with cancer.

Rosie was Mom's dog and only Mom's dog. She did not need other people in her life, and her eyes were always on Mom. A black wolf-like dog, Rosie was very internal and kept to herself; we did not see much of her unless we were with Mom. I never really connected with Rosie.

When Rosie was dying, Mom was devastated.

Interestingly, Rosie had cancer all over her body, and some of the tumors were visible just like Mom's were. One of Rosie's tumors on her leg was giant and open, and Mom tended to it and to Rosie with grace.

It became clear that Rosie was struggling. Her tumors were starting to bleed heavily and it was close to her end, so Mom called her vets and called me and we all went to Mom's house. It was time to put Rosie to sleep.

Because I had a little detachment from Rosie, I was able to be there in a different way than I would have been if she and I were close. I felt sad for Mom, and I felt sad for Rosie, but I also felt a little more removed. Because of this, I was able to watch what happened from a different perspective.

I could tell Rosie knew what was coming and was ready. She had the giant tumor for a long while, and it seemed like she had come to terms with her illness. She felt at peace to me.

I was not looking to see energy; I was just present holding the space for her and for Mom.

The vet said they would first give her a sedative to relax her and then they would give her the medicine that put her to sleep.

As Rosie was relaxing deeply with the sedative, I saw an energy that looked like a mixture of mist and smoke gathering over her body. I blinked, because the energy was so visible to me. It was still there so I just observed it. It gathered over her body and then gathered at the top of her head and just before the vet said, "She's gone," I saw it poof out of the top of her head and fill the room with sparkling light and a feeling of expansive peace.

Of course, Mom was devastated. We said goodbye to Rosie's body and the vets took her away to be cremated.

I told Mom what I had seen, and we sat together in the room feeling the energy of Rosie's spirit. I was awestruck by what I had experienced. Previously, I had mostly seen energy internally in my mind's eye, but with Rosie what I saw was as clear as I saw the clouds in the sky.

From what I had witnessed, I knew she was with us and I felt she was at peace. Because grief is such a dense array of emotions, Mom didn't feel Rosie the way I could. It did bring her some peace to know I could feel Rosie, but I do not know that she fully understood the life-altering effect Rosie had on me.

Rosie's passing gave me an immense perspective on death. I will be forever grateful to her for that because she helped me see and feel the soul leave the body. This prepared me for many loses that followed, but it especially helped me when Mom died. The grief was too thick for me to see Mom's energy, but I knew it was there, thanks to Rosie.

Chapter Twenty-Nine

The Day of the Dead

It was clear that Mom's cancer was taking over, and it was also clear that her body couldn't take more treatment. After she got out of the hospital and Chris and Abby brought her mind back from wandering, the doctors decided to take her off of chemo for a while in order for her body to recover. She was never able to tolerate the chemo again.

There were two beautiful months where Mom had less chemo brain. We blamed all of Mom's cognitive issues on the chemo, and most of the time that allowed us to laugh through her mind's misadventures. "Chemo brain," we'd say with a chuckle when she got stuck in a sentence she couldn't finish. As much as we laughed about it, chemo brain was a frustration for all of us along the way. It made Mom's mind muddy.

During this respite from chemo, an extra part of her awareness came back, which was a silver lining in the midst of the reality that her cancer was not being treated and was most likely spreading.

One of our last adventures together was going to a Day of the Dead celebration in Albuquerque called the Marigold Parade.

Before cancer, Mom had often avoided going out and doing things and tended to isolate herself. She would say she was tired, or she would have vague illnesses. It felt like she was disengaged from life and people.

Once she had cancer, she jumped at every chance to live, so she wanted to go to the Marigold Parade. My friend Annie was an honorary daughter to Mom and is a soul sister of mine. She was often the one to come along for our forays into the world, and this day was no exception.

It was always a lot of work to take Mom out. We had to consider if she could walk. If so, we brought the walker. If not, we brought her wheelchair. We had to make sure she didn't get mowed down in big crowds because people very often don't pay attention to wheelchairs and fragile people.

That day, Mom was shining from the inside and her joy was tangible. Annie does face painting for kids, and we all painted our faces like sugar skulls, which is the tradition on the Day of the Dead. Our faces were white to look like a skeleton, with colorful flowers and images adorning the white. Today was a wheelchair day, and we wheeled Mom down to the parade.

It was incredibly meaningful to be at a parade with Mom to honor the people who had passed before us. It was a happy celebration and everyone was dressed to honor the dead. There were floats filled with flowers and sugar skulls that were radiating love. I knew in my heart that this would be our last time to do this together and that the following year, I would go to remember Mom with everyone who was memorializing those who they had lost. It was a bit surreal but also heartwarming.

That day, a family took Mom under their wings and got her right to the front of the crowd. They gathered around us and protected us like we were one of their own. A woman with slicked-back hair and a strong demeanor gave Mom a big smile and a top hat with a rose to shade her from the sun.

"Rosie's saying hello," Mom said.

The incredible and kind family would not let anyone knock into us, and Mom made fast friends with a little girl with sticky fingers who shared her candy with Mom.

Part of the parade was filled with lowriders, and we smiled with delight as they went by bouncing and using their hydraulics.

While the parade was passing through, I took a deep breath and soaked in the energy from the crowd and the experience of sharing this with Mom. Being present was all I could do to activate the feeling of expansive love and joy in my heart and hope that I could capture that feeling along the way after I lost her.

I can feel the love I felt that day and it brings tears of joy to my eyes. Emotional experiences are never truly lost. They are embedded in the very fiber of our being.

Chapter Thirty

Caught Between a Rock and a Hard Place

In the next month, Mom and I went to see the birds down in the Bosque del Apache a lot. We went to eat at all of her favorite restaurants. We went to listen to live music. We continued to do all of her favorite things.

One night, I got a terrible stomach virus. I was fine one minute and throwing up the next. It came out of nowhere and happened simultaneously with Mom taking a bad fall. This demonstrates how connected we are with those we love. It also shows how we feel something in our body. I felt the beginning of the end for Mom, and it made me violently ill.

This brings to attention something I have been wanting to talk about: the beauty of a team of people who help through thick and thin.

Through Mom's illness, I had a few core people who saved my life and Mom's over and over again. They spent time with Mom so

I could have sanity breaks. They were our guardian angels here on earth and helped on a moment's notice.

They went to the grocery store, took Mom to her radiation treatments, took her to movies and meals, and sat with her when I couldn't.

Since Mom was in and out of the hospital every couple of months for a few years, without my friends I would have probably wound up in an insane asylum, or sick myself. They would give me breaks so I could go get food or walk my dogs or just get out of the hospital and breathe fresh air.

So when Mom fell and I was incapacitated with the stomach flu, I called my friends Betsy and Paul, and they went with Mom to the hospital for me.

Loyce, Annie, Jan, Julie, Betsy, and Paul took turns being there with her all day, and they reported what the doctors said while I was getting well.

Mom was discharged that day and was sore. Little did we know that her cancer was starting to break her bones again. A couple of nights later, she was moving in her bed and felt a pop. She broke her hip lying in bed.

She didn't have her phone, her emergency alert, or her talker near her when it happened. I had seen her struggling a bit in her monitor but then it looked like she was restful. She had to spend the entire night in agony with a broken hip and no help.

She said she spent the night knowing she was dying—knowing this was it. She sat with the grief of it and sat with the physical pain, and she sat with all of it alone.

This was her final night in her apartment.

I got a call from her nurse the next morning saying that Mom couldn't get out of bed. I arrived, and it was clear that there was something really wrong. She couldn't put any weight on her leg, so I called the paramedics. Soon there were five men and women crowded in her room taking her vitals and assessing her condition. There was an unreality to it all. The confusion, the pain, and also the kindness of all the people who were there to help was overwhelming. Mom was given strong medication so she could be transferred from her bed to a stretcher. She grimaced as they lifted her, but the gentleness from these strong and healthy people who were moving her was a touching sight. She was wheeled through the sterile hallways to an ambulance.

We left her apartment in total disarray. Life changed yet again in an instant.

The doctors gave us the option of a hip replacement, which seemed ridiculous, or to leave it broken, which also seemed ridiculous. No one was giving us an indication of how long she had to live, but living with a broken hip seemed like it would cause her agony if she lived very long.

She chose to have the surgery. She didn't want to lie there with a broken hip waiting to die.

I was Mom's medical power of attorney. What a role to have to play for someone. My goal at the end of Mom's life was to support what she wanted for herself, not to do what I would want. That was much easier said than done.

It would have been easy to project my own ideas and beliefs on Mom's dying process. My goal was to keep the "I" out of the equation and look to who she was and what she wanted. There was no perfect way of doing that other than to talk to her and to listen as much as I could along the way.

Up to this point, Mom had never signed a DNR, do not resuscitate. Every time we had gone to the hospital, she had wanted to be revived if possible. This time felt different, so I sat her down and said, "Mom, you are dying. I don't feel like you can beat this any longer. I think you need to sign a DNR."

This conversation would have been unheard of for her up until now.

"I agree," Mom said, "I spent the whole night thinking about it, and it feels like I am really dying now."

"I'm so sorry, Mom, this is so hard."

"It is. I just didn't want this time to come. I wanted to beat this. I wanted to live."

"I know. I wanted that too."

We just sat together and felt the gravity.

She signed the DNR.

I didn't know if Mom's body could withstand the surgery. She was wasting away from the cancer, and as tough as she was, it seemed kind of impossible.

Aunt Betty had flown to Albuquerque on the day Mom broke her hip. She was just coming for a visit and got a call from me to meet us at the hospital.

She put on a brave face when she walked into the room and saw Mom; the love they felt for each other was tangible. There were tears in both of their eyes as they courageously discussed the reality of this moment.

I left them so they could have time together.

The next day, Aunt Betty and I sat with Mom all morning before surgery talking about our lives. The surgery kept getting pushed back, and we magically wound up with the whole day together.

Aunt Betty and Mom had been close throughout the years. They traveled all over the country with their parents as kids and had gotten into mischief wherever they went.

"Hey little rabbits," my dad said as he turned in his seat to look at me and Betty, "let's sing some songs."

We were sweltering in the heat and bored to tears from the long car ride but that got us, all right. My dad sensed that it would. Before we knew it, we were all singing, "You Are My Sunshine" at the top of our lungs.

And that's when it happened. All of a sudden, just as we sang, "You make me happy when skies are gray," the wind in the car caught Dad's favorite fishing hat. It sailed past Mom in the passenger seat and flew right out her window.

"My hat," Dad groaned, sounding as if he had lost the meaning of his existence.

Betty and I scrambled to look out the back of our station wagon, excited by something for the first time that afternoon. We were happy, by golly, that something was actually happening.

Dad couldn't slam on the breaks right away because of all of the traffic and shouted, "Count all of the telephone polls so we'll know how far back to go!"

And we did. 12, 15, 18, 25, 35. By then we were so far that Dad decided to make a U-turn. When we found a place to turn around, we counted backward to the spot.

We all shot out of the car, and we walked up and down the side of the road for fifteen minutes or more.

"Maybe we counted wrong," said Mom.

"Maybe we need to go farther from the road," Dad said as he tried to figure out the trajectory of the hat.

We looked and looked for the hat, but it was nowhere to be seen. We were whipped.

We all dragged ourselves back to the car, my dad in the lead disheartened that he had lost the meaning of his existence out on that lonely, hot road in Southern Wyoming. I looked up at our car just ahead and there the hat was hanging on the outside handle of Mom's door. It was hanging there as easygoing, as lopsided as it had always been. Hanging there for all the whole world to see. Hanging there the entire time we had been traipsing up and down that highway.

We'd lost his hat before. He'd leave it on the table in a restaurant and we'd have to drive a half an hour back to get it. It drove us crazy, but oh, what I would give to have just one of those blessed days back. All of us driving through the scorching summer heat, laughing, singing songs and happy because Dad had once again gotten his fishing hat back.

The stories they told that day were filled with laughter and tears. We got out my phone and sang along to all of our favorite songs. Mom's robot voice was loud and brave yet again during a rough and scary circumstance.

Annie came to be with me while Mom had surgery, and we spent a Friday night at the hospital waiting to hear what happened. Mom made it through the surgery, and we sat with her while she woke up. She was groggy but strong as she came through anesthesia, and we could see that she still had the fire inside to live.

The number of hours it was going to take every day to navigate Mom's rapidly evolving health issues was overwhelming, so my cousin Peter came to support us. He, Aunt Betty, and Mom listened to Bob Dylan, laughed together, and told tall tales. Peter and Aunt Betty left after a week with tears, knowing this was likely the last time they would see Mom.

Death doesn't come easily for some. Mom was one of those people. She loved so fiercely and wanted so clearly to stay with us all forever. Spirit be damned at that moment, she dug in and lived for another month and a half after surgery.

This began a long road to Mom's final resting place.

Chapter Thirty-One

The Last Goodbyes

Mom's hip surgery was December 15, 2018. It's a little bit of a blur what happened from there. While Aunt Betty and Peter were with us, we enlisted Mom's doctor from palliative care to join her team.

Aunt Linda arrived at some point to help me because someone needed to be at the hospital all day and much of the night. Mom was failing and it was uncertain how much time she had. My friends visited and gave both Aunt Linda and me breathers, sat with Mom, and were also available to talk to the doctors.

When Aunt Linda left, there were tears in her eyes, knowing that this was likely to be the last time she got to see Mom.

It was clear Mom was struggling. Her vitals were weak, she was disoriented, and she occasionally dropped into a deep sleep and couldn't be woken up. Her doctor called me and told me to get anyone to Albuquerque who would want to say goodbye because she felt like the time of Mom's passing was near.

I called my brother and he booked a ticket to come that day.

Right before he flew in, the doctors called me and said to get to Mom's side immediately because they thought Mom might be dying. When I got there, she was in a deep and peaceful coma.

Mike arrived to a somber scene and was relieved that Mom was still with us. He decided to sleep in the hospital room with Mom so he could be there in case she declined in the night.

At some point in the middle of the night, Mom started using her talker. She woke up from her coma worried about doing her laundry, and the two of them laughed.

It was a surprise for Mike to get to talk with her, and he seized the moment to share stories and memories and laughter together. Her mind kept wandering into the need to do her laundry, and she would get a funny smile on her face realizing she was in the hospital and there was no laundry to do. They shared a meaningful couple of days together.

At one point, an orderly brought Mom her dinner, and she looked down at it and said with disdain, "Fuckin' chicken."

Mike started laughing and said, "Mom, do you want me to bring you something fun to eat?"

"Yes!" she said emphatically and he got her a giant chocolate chip cookie ice cream sandwich. For the rest of their time together, he brought her some of her favorite foods: breakfast burritos, spring rolls and Pho, and milkshakes.

Mike's presence brought Mom back, and she became engaged in life again.

While Mom's body was breaking down from the cancer, my house started falling apart. My water heater broke, my dishwasher broke, my washing machine broke, and my front door lock stopped working. It was as if my house was mirroring what was happening for Mom. I was scrambling to deal with all of the extra challenges.

Mike flew home to be with the kids for Christmas, and my dad flew in on Christmas Eve to support me. Aunt Betty had decorated Mom's room with a little twirling tree that played "Jingle Bells," and Annie bought her a snowflake light. It was as cheerful as it could be, but it felt sad to experience the holiday in the hospital watching my mom slowly letting go of life.

My friend Julie sat with Mom Christmas morning so that I could gather my energy to celebrate. To cheer Mom and me up, I dressed in a ridiculous Christmas outfit. I had a fuzzy white sweater with a glittery penguin on it and a Santa hat that said "Merry Elfin' Christmas" and blinked with green and red lights. Mom laughed when I got there and wanted to take a picture of me. At this point, the bones in her shoulders were broken from the cancer in them so I had to stoop low to get in the shot. We played holiday songs on my phone while she and I gently held hands and sang and "danced." It was a bittersweet holiday, but very special.

While he was visiting, Dad got to spend time with Mom reminiscing and telling stories. After he left the room, I asked Mom how it went and she smiled. She said very well, and I could see the healing that had happened in Mom. Her demeanor indicated that she had forgiven Dad and felt at peace with him. It brought tears to my eyes. My dad was touched as well and his heart was heavy when he left, knowing that this was the last time he would see her.

There were multiple times in those weeks in the hospital when they called me into the room and told me she was dying, but she kept pulling through. It seemed like she might be waiting to say goodbye to the people she loved, and each person she said goodbye to left in tears.

Mike and Kim brought Chris and Abby the day after Christmas and planned to stay for a week to be with Mom. The hospital gave special permission for the kids to see her. This had been the first Christmas since the kids were born that Mom wasn't with them in Seattle.

The interesting thing I kept discovering and being surprised by was that Mom lived on love. When she saw Chris and Abby, she kicked into gear again and became more awake and alive. The doctors stopped calling me in to say goodbye.

We realized that she would live longer than we had expected, so Mike and Kim found her a new facility and we started to look at her living days, possibly weeks, instead of minutes and hours.

She transferred to her new facility, and this allowed the kids to be with her because there weren't restrictions around children. We bought paints, and the kids and Mom painted lots of pictures and got to spend some quality time with each other.

On New Year's Eve, they all flew back home to Seattle. Before their departure, each of them sat with Mom saying what would likely be their final goodbye. It was emotionally intense for all of them, and I sat in the lobby as each one of them came out looking shattered.

Mike had a connection to Mom as deep as mine. They were best friends and loved each other completely, and there was a likelihood that he would never see her again.

How do you say goodbye? It is devastatingly hard.

It felt unreal because Mom always seemed to pull through, but we all realized she couldn't pull through forever. We were all quiet at dinner after we left her. We all felt the weight of the moment, and we picked at our food.

We faced a new year that would likely be without Mom.

Chapter Thirty-Two

One Person's Heaven Is Another Person's Hell

The skilled nursing facility that Mike and Kim found for Mom was a familiar place. It was the same facility where a best friend of mine named Emily had died when she was ninety-five.

While I was learning to practice and teach Reiki in the mid-nineties, my mentor introduced me to Emily because Emily had arthritis and Reiki helped her feel better. I went to her house and gave her weekly sessions, and we soon became fast friends. Emily had clear blue eyes that pierced into your soul, tight curls on the top of her head, a contagious laugh, and she either liked you or distrusted you immediately. I was lucky to be someone she liked because she was an exceptional friend.

I called Emily "Mama" because we once went to an Italian restaurant, and a male opera singer came over to us and sang a loud opera song about Mama, and Emily had fallen in love with the song and the man and the whole experience.

Mom was never very happy about me calling Emily "Mama," so I started calling Mom "Mamacita" so she wouldn't feel left out.

Emily was born a cowgirl in Cloudcroft, New Mexico. Even now, Cloudcroft is like stepping back in time onto a movie set from the Old West. She rode a horse everywhere she went, and she hunted elk for her family's dinner. At an early age, she started cutting hair to help support her family and went from home to home on her horse; she was a traveling beautician. As you can imagine, she was strong-willed and fun and had great stories.

Emily was tough, but she was also sensitive and very perceptive of energy. She would talk about having tingling sensations in her mind when someone was thinking of her, and then that person would call her that day. She would feel it if someone was angry or happy with her.

We were good buddies, and we did everything from Reiki to going to breakfast to drinking gin because she was convinced that gin mixed with raisins would cure arthritis.

When Mom moved to Albuquerque she became fast friends with Emily as well, and we all had good times together.

As Emily moved toward the end of her life, she started hearing people singing outside of her house.

"Liz, these people are driving me nuts! They're outside my house every night singing 'Amazing Grace'! You need to come over and tell them to leave."

Sure enough, I would go to her house and there was no one there.

"They must be spirits coming to sing to you, Mama . . . You're going to have to tell them to stop in your mind."

Emily had been in a band when she was younger and had played the fiddle. Her husband had been in trouble with the law, and she had some wild stories about escaping from the police with him.

"Maybe it's some of your friends in heaven saying hi to you," I said.

"Well, I sure wish they would be quiet," Emily said back to me in her Southern twang of an accent.

We went for a drive one day, and she saw a man doing somersaults in front of us and goofing around; she asked if I could see him. I said no.

"Do you recognize him?" I asked and she said no.

These visitations from spirit or hallucinations made her a little agitated, even though I found them fascinating. It seemed like her divine friends were trying to get her attention and she was wanting to ignore them. Emily stubbornly wanted to live forever.

Not long after, she had a fall and wound up in the same skilled nursing facility Mom ended up in ten years later. This nursing home was the kind you might have nightmares about; there was a lot of neglect. They lost Emily's hearing aids and never replaced them. She fell a couple of times while she was there. I would find her in a wheelchair making noises that sounded like a sheep. It made me sad for her.

I would visit and shout to her so she could hear me, "Go to the angels!" I felt like since she was dying, she might as well go as fast as she could to get out of this situation. I always wondered what people thought when they heard me shouting.

One day, while I was there to see Emily, her roommate had a visitor. Previously, I had seen her roommate looking checked-out and unhappy as she tried to move around the facility in a wheelchair.

The visitor that day was a nurse assessing her condition. I couldn't help but listen because we were in the same room only separated by a sheet and they were talking loudly.

"Do you know your name?" the nurse asked.

"Yes, ma'am."

"What is it?"

She said her name and then said ma'am again.

"Do you know the year?"

"Yes, ma'am."

"What is it?"

She said the year and then said ma'am again.

This went on for a while with all of the mundane questions that people need to answer for an assessment. She was answering all of the questions right. But then it got interesting.

"Do you know where you are?"

"Yes, ma'am."

"Where are you?"

And this woman said very clearly in a more alert tone of voice, "Heaven."

I sat to attention, because I was looking around this place feeling sorry for everyone there and feeling like it was hell.

The nurse sounded shocked as well and asked again, "*Where* are you?"

"Heaven, ma'am."

Here I was thinking Emily needed to die to be in heaven, but heaven was right here right now. Her *body* was going through the process of dying, but that didn't necessarily mean that her *being* suffered.

I realized that something transcendental happens in the dying process. Those of us who are not dying see the body dying. It is a hard thing to witness because the body is taught to survive, and when it breaks down it is not pretty.

What we see is only part of the picture.

Emily's roommate gave me such a gift. She reminded me that we are not just our bodies. We are spiritual beings having a physical experience. We can experience heaven even when our life looks like hell.

Thank goodness I had gained this knowledge from Emily and her roommate before I got to a similar place with Mom. It helped me see a bigger picture while I was watching Mom in her dying process, and it helped me know that a part of her was here, but a part of her was having a divine experience at the same time.

Emily died a few weeks later, but I stopped trying to tell her to go. I simply sat with her when I visited and held a space of love for the life that she lived and for the friendship that we shared.

Mom and Emily both bestowed on me a love for being human. They did not take letting go of this life lightly, and they held on to this experience until their final breath. They taught me that there is more than meets the eye when it comes to dying and to be patient with the process, even though it felt unbearable at times.

They woke me up to the understanding that a life filled with love is not easy to leave and that death has its own time and its own way.

Chapter Thirty-Three

Do Not Go Gentle into That Good Night

I would like to update everyone on how I have been. As you know, I have a rare thyroid cancer. I've been on chemo and it worked for a long while but now it stopped working. I am trying to find peace with my mortality. I don't know how long I have. Some days are hard and some days I am able to find peace. Three weeks ago, I fractured my hip because I have cancer in my bones. It is difficult to not be able to walk and I am at a rehab clinic. I send you all my love and I would appreciate any prayers for peace that you can send me.

We die how we live.

In my years of doing healing work, I have supported many people and animals through the dying process. Whether it be their own death or the death of someone they love, I have witnessed a multitude of different ways of dying.

There are those who go in their sleep without fanfare, some who go with massive pain and suffering, and some who go in between the two extremes. Every death is unique to the one who is dying.

I recently sat with a dog who was dying. He was a handsome Doberman named Buddy who had lived until he was fourteen, which is rare for such a big dog. He had a serious and dignified demeanor, and I had become good friends with him over "puppucinos" from Starbucks. This is basically an espresso cup filled with whipped cream, and what dog wouldn't enjoy that, even the serious kind?

It was clear that it was his time. He could no longer eat, stand up, or walk, so his mom and I sat with him and gave him Reiki to keep him comfortable while he was dying.

As awful as it was to know that my friend was losing someone so dear to her, there was still the overwhelming feeling of love and beauty surrounding him while he was dying. As the body shuts down, the spirit is powerfully present, and the preparation for the soul's leaving has an illuminated feel to it.

While sitting with Buddy, I was reminded of the sacredness of supporting someone in dying their own way. His mom knew him so well and held the space for him. She was able to bring in the veterinarian when it became clear that he was suffering, and he was able to be put to sleep at his house in a peaceful way.

He died in the gentlemanly way that he lived.

I think back to Mom and to supporting her in her dying process. I kept having to check in with what *she* would want instead of trying to impose myself on the equation. There were a lot of curious decisions I had to make in order to create the best possible space for her to go.

The last two months of Mom's life were a struggle for her. She knew she was dying, but she was confused a lot as well, so I often had to make decisions for her.

While she was at Emily's nursing home she seemed happy and content and said that she liked the place. She may have been experiencing an internal "heaven," but it was a very neglectful place. I would walk in and she would be covered with food because she couldn't feed herself and no one helped her, or they would forget to give her an important medication. I had to be there most of the day to make sure she had the care she needed.

After about a week, she was re-admitted to the hospital because the nurses were incapable of suctioning her so she could breathe. There was a plug in her trach and she was barely getting any oxygen. She had developed pneumonia because of the lack of care.

It was the last time Mom was sent to the hospital.

I had been out with some friends at a fancy restaurant for a birthday gathering. Annie came with me to the hospital, and we were wearing our finest clothes. Mom's insurance always took her to the county hospital, which was an intense experience every time. There were patients with knife wounds walking around groaning and bleeding, people withdrawing from drugs, and long rows of folks sniffing and sneezing all over everyone. On this occasion, they took us to a private room and let us wait there until I could see Mom. It made me realize that it would have been useful to dress up all of those years I had been going to the ER because they treated me differently when I did.

All that aside, there were two choices for Mom's care. One was to treat the pneumonia with a heavy antibiotic and admit her to the hospital, and the other was to send her back to the facility with more of a hospice approach.

Mom was not in hospice at the time because she couldn't be in hospice and also be in rehab due to her insurance policy. Hospice is only there to make people comfortable as they are dying, and she would not be able to receive any rehabilitation with hospice.

Mom wanted to keep moving and continue to receive physical therapy. We knew she was dying, she knew she was dying, but she kept choosing to live as well as she could while she was dying. This was her choice and her way of dealing with her situation. We had consulted with hospice, and they were on call for Mom whenever she was ready to stop rehab.

Because Mom was not in hospice, it looked on paper like we were unaware of what was going on. So, while I was at the hospital dressed in my finest clothes, the team of young doctors sat me down and told me Mom was dying, as though this was new information for me. It would have been comical if it wasn't so tragic.

I explained that I knew and that this was Mom's wish to keep living as well as she could while she was dying.

I also explained that I would not agree to send Mom back to the facility that she had been in because they were incapable of taking care of her.

While I write this, I think of mothers and how they fight for their kids. I felt like this for Mom. She had fought for me throughout her life, and now it was time for me to be there for her. I would stand up for her no matter what it took to create the best space for her to die, even if I wound up looking dumb in order to convince other people to support her in the way she wanted.

We agreed that the best decision was to admit her to the hospital to treat the pneumonia and in the meantime find her a new facility.

From that choice, I got a lot of questions from the doctors who seemed to think I was unaware of Mom's situation, and I continually had a barrage of people sitting me down and explaining to me that my mother was dying.

"No kidding," I wanted to say, but I patiently explained Mom's wishes and my choices that were all meant to support those wishes. I also had to explain the level of neglect at the facility where she was previously a patient. This is when Mom's doctor who worked in palliative care came in and supported us. She knew Mom's history, she knew me, and she helped us find solutions.

She and her team were able to talk with all of the doctors and coordinate the plan to move Mom to a better skilled nursing facility.

When Mom was released from the hospital to the facility where she ultimately died, I had a palliative care nurse tell me that she admired the way I was honoring my mom and what she needed. It was nice to have that acknowledgment.

I realized later that Mom dealt with a similar process when it came to honoring her dad's wishes when he died.

The hardest thing in my life was to find out that my dad had cancer and then knowing that he was going to pass away. My dad had a special place in my heart and this was a sad, stressful time. I had a hard time admitting that he was going to die and, quite frankly, I didn't handle it very well. One time my dad was in his hospital room with the shades drawn and the door closed. I came in and tried to cheer him up and opened the blinds. I later realized that I should have left him alone or joined him in the dark and cried with him.

I remember Mom telling me this story along the way in my life, and it had stuck with me and helped me be there for her in *her* way when she was dying.

It was a struggle to work through my own ideas of what I would want in Mom's situation, the doctor's opinions, and all of Mom's and my friends and family who had opinions about what they would do. Finding Mom's truth in the midst of that was perplexing, and I felt like I had to fight for the space to hear her truth.

I'm very certain I didn't choose perfectly along the way, but I'm also certain I did pretty well by Mom.

All this said, when it is possible, it feels important to create the space for each person to die in their own way. There is no standard way to live, and there is likewise no standard way to die.

I also know that people can be scared when they are dying, and it can be difficult to understand their needs and support them. I was lucky with Mom that we had such an extensive understanding of each other and that she was willing to have me be there for her in every way I could.

Mom loved the poem "Do Not Go Gentle into That Good Night" by Dylan Thomas.

Do not go gentle into that good night,
Old age should burn and rave at close of day;
Rage, rage against the dying of the light.

I always thought of Mom as squeezing out every last drop of life she could. She fought to live every possible moment, even if it caused her suffering. It was worth it to her.

It was her life.

It was her death.

Chapter Thirty-Four

The Life of the Party

When Mom and I talked about dying, one of her biggest struggles was with leaving the party. She didn't want to miss out on all of the fun she knew existed in life. She saw life as a party. Seeing her grandkids grow up. Seeing my brother and me evolve. Writing her novel. Talking with her sister and the rest of her family. Hearing from her friends. Going on adventures. Seeing the world progress. Life was a celebration that she would love to continue until eternity.

The day I knew Mom was actively starting to die was while we were in the hospital her last time and she was about to be transferred to her final skilled nursing facility.

I walked into her room in the morning and her eyes lit up.

Something felt different and new. She had lost the anxiety that was always present in the midst of all of her inspiration and love of life.

"You're here to join the party," she said with her talker.

"I am," I said.

At this point, her body was being crushed. Her bones were breaking from the cancer inside of them. She had every reason to be in agony in her body and in her heart, but instead she was happy and at a party.

Mom was very clearly somewhere else in her heart and mind. She was looking around and seeing people and smiling. The nurses would come to bring her food and drinks and she would ask them if they were having fun. I told them we were at a party and they all laughed and said, "Great!"

Mom told me she was wearing a purple dress and that the party had interesting people she didn't know but really liked. She was joyful the whole day, and when the nurses came to turn her so she didn't get bedsores, she would smile like they were dancing with her.

We talked and reminisced and had a sweet day at the party together.

My heart felt happy and sad at the same time. Finally she could see that there was a party where she was going. I feel like the divine showed her a party to help her to realize that the celebrations would continue when she died. I knew death was happening for her and that she would soon be able to let go.

Out of curiosity, I asked a nurse if she could explain what was going on physically. Was it the drugs? Was it the dying process? She said that this kind of thing happened sometimes but the reason remained a mystery.

I was honored to be in this mysterious in-between world with Mom. I felt souls all around us who would greet her when she died, and I was with the people here in this world who held the space for her to die. What a sacred place.

Even though I had known death was coming for Mom, it was still crushing to get to this point. I was ready for Mom's suffering to be over. I was ready for her to be at peace. But I would never truly be ready to let her go.

That day she was being transferred from the hospital to what would wind up being her final resting place.

Usually when she was transferred to a new place, she would be filled with anxiety and confusion. But on this day when they came to pick her up she was happy and thought she was getting a ride home from her party.

When I arrived to meet her at the new facility, her eyes were wide and she told me that she had a wild ride! She was convinced that she was in Madison, Wisconsin, and that they had driven like wildfire all the way home. The ride of her life, she said. And it turned out to be the last ride of her life. Those drivers had no idea what a final thrill they gave Mom.

The day after Mom's party, I went to be with her. We had our own room, which proved to be miraculous for all of us who wanted to sit with her while she was dying.

I was feeding her because of her broken shoulders. She couldn't eat by herself, but Mom absolutely loved to eat and didn't mind being fed. Once again, it felt like a role reversal and a passing of the baton. She had fed me as a child, and I was getting to give her the same love.

She acted confused about where she was, but was also content in her confusion. For conversation, I asked her if she could be anywhere in the world, where would she like to be? We always enjoyed daydreaming about traveling to the many places we had been and the many places we would like to go.

Today, though, was different. She looked me in the eye said, *"Right here."*

When she looked at me I felt our souls connect and time stand still.

"Right here?" I asked.

"Yes," she said and smiled at me sweetly.

This was mind-blowing for Mom, because she was always seeking in life—seeking a new experience, a new thought. For her to be content to be right here in this skilled nursing facility meant that she had truly found peace. To me this was enlightenment.

I told her that I wanted to be right here, too, and we just sat and smiled at each other for a while.

While she was smiling at me and studying me, she said, "I hope I remember you."

"Remember me when you die?" I asked.

"Yes."

"You will," I said and she smiled.

My heart broke open with the profound realization that I needed to study her face and her energy and let it imprint on my soul. Not that it hadn't before, but I felt the need to be more conscious of absorbing the energy between us so that we would forever know each other at a soul level.

We both spent time that day just being with each other and adding a layer of consciousness to the connection we had.

Later that day, Mom and I were talking again.

"Liz, I think I am dying," she said.

"Right now?" I asked.

"Maybe."

"Is it scary or is it peaceful?" I asked.

"Both."

"Is it more scary or more peaceful?"

"Scary," she said.

I asked her if she could turn her focus to the peaceful feeling, and I could see her do that in her mind. Her face became tranquil and she fell asleep.

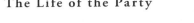

She woke up a little while later and mouthed, "Death is peaceful," and then fell back asleep.

That night, Mom had a full-blown panic attack. She must have started to let herself die and then she got scared. She was wide awake with her eyes unfocused looking out at someone or something, and she was mouthing "no, no, no, no," over and over again and shaking her head. She wasn't hearing me or seeing me and nothing I could say would calm her down.

I thought this was the moment of death, but the nurses told me that her vitals were not indicating that she was dying, so we gave her medicine to calm her down and I just had to sit with her and wait out the panic attack. After about five hours, she was finally able to close her eyes and get to sleep, but it was her final fight to live and she fought with all of her might.

The next day she was peaceful again. It was the day before my birthday and she sang me "Happy Birthday" and we ate cake. People visited and we had a memorable day where we all sang songs and talked and prayed. She didn't seem to be worried about where she was or what was happening. She had let go of the fight.

This was the day we set up hospice for Mom. It was time to support her in fully letting go and to make her as comfortable as possible along the way. This is a charged choice for a lot of people, but all of us who loved Mom, including Mom herself, had considered her to be on hospice for a long time, so this was just a formality for us.

I arrived at the facility on my birthday; she was non-responsive and had slipped into a coma. Julie came and sat with her so Jan, Annie, and I could get out and process the gravity of what was happening.

I walked back into the room on my final birthday with my incredible Mom and tears welled in my eyes.

I cried and sat with her most of the day, playing guitar and singing to her, saying prayers, and just being with her. At one point in the day, she opened her eyes and mouthed "I love you" and made kisses in the air and then went back out.

I thought this was it, that she would go.

I asked Annie to take the next day off of work so she could be with me because I thought Mom would likely die that day.

When we arrived that morning, she was wide awake and ready for breakfast. It was such a shock, my jaw dropped open and stayed that way for most of the day,

"What are we going to dress like for Halloween?" she asked. (It was January, but Mom, Annie, and I loved planning our Halloween costumes.)

"Mom, you were in a coma yesterday! I am so shocked and happy that you are talking!"

"I was?" she asked.

Then she asked for breakfast.

"Do you remember anything about where you were?" I asked.

"Not really," she said. "I might remember music."

She ate her whole breakfast.

Loyce came in thinking she was going to find Mom in a coma, and her jaw dropped open as well. The three of us sat dumbstruck as Mom asked us to go get her a decaf soy latte which she sucked down with enthusiasm.

I knew this day was a gift and also knew that it was most likely the last wind that people talk about when someone is dying.

I didn't realize when I had heard about it from other people how shocking it would feel. It was the best present I could ever receive. To be able to talk to Mom for the last time when I already felt like I had talked with her for the last time was amazing.

We considered Halloween costumes, I played guitar, we sang all of the songs I know, and we talked about everything and nothing. My sister-in-law Kim flew in and we all laughed together, and Mom downed the largest chocolate milkshake you have ever seen. It turned out to be her last meal.

She was so happy. She had one last party. And now she could really rest and let go.

Chapter Thirty-Five

The Fated Moment

It's hard to write about the very end of Mom's life. It was such an emotionally devastating time. As I sit here writing, tears begin to fall. I can imagine that even if I were to write this ten years from now, tears would also begin to fall. How do I express the loss of someone so important to me?

In the five years Mom was ill, we had multiple goodbyes because there were multiple times she could have died. There was an unreality to the moment we had come to because Mom had always pulled through. I had seen Mom incredibly weak physically and mentally, and I had seen her become strong again. She had in many ways died and come back to life a plethora (one of Mom's favorite words) of times.

Knowing this was it was an impossible thing to grasp.

A good friend had asked me a few times, "Are you ready for your mom to die? Are you prepared?" She had lost both of her parents and a sister so she knew what was coming for me.

I kept saying, "I am as ready as I can be."

In reality, I couldn't fully prepare myself for that kind of loss. I couldn't feel what it would be like to live without Mom until she actually died. Then I dealt with it the best I could.

After Mom had her full day of coming back to life, she fell back into a coma again and never woke up.

Of course, life continues on in the midst of challenges, and I had to finish moving her stuff out of her independent living apartment the day she went back into the coma. Kim sat with Mom while some friends and I moved her belongings.

We moved everything out of her apartment, did a final sweep to make sure we got it all, and Jan and I sat on the floor and did a prayer.

In the prayer I said something like, "Thank you for this beautiful home. Thank you for housing my mom and supporting her in living a good life at the end of her life. I call in Mom's soul and ask that she know that she has moved and that she can now be free. She can let go of this life knowing that she has lived well and that she is no longer tethered to her house, to her things, and to this community. May this space be blessed with the love and laughter and life she experienced here, Amen."

The minute I finished the prayer, I got a phone call from the hospice nurse.

"You need to get here right now. Your mom is dying."

Mom's oxygen levels had begun to drop just as I was doing the prayer.

The hospice nurse and I didn't know each other well at this point, so she didn't know about the bond Mom and I shared.

I had conversations with Mom before she had gone into a coma. I told her I felt like I might not be able to be there with her when she died. I was worried that she might not be able to let go of this life if

I was in the room with her and she had agreed. I also had told Mom over the years of her dying process that if she felt like she was dying, that she should let go. I would be okay and I didn't want her to hold on to life because of me.

I didn't want to cause Mom to prolong her life if that would bring her any suffering, but I went when the hospice nurse called me because I wanted to say goodbye.

I entered the room and held Mom's hand and prayed for her to pass peacefully and to let go. The monitor showing Mom's oxygen levels began to rise right before our eyes. The nurse's mouth dropped open. Her oxygen levels went to normal in about a minute, and then the monitor went blank and they were never able to get a read on her oxygen again. Mom began to live off of the ethers.

The nurse told me then that 80 percent of people died when their loved ones were out of the room, so we started to make a conscious effort to give Mom space to die while also being there to support her.

Mike wanted to be there, but we realized he would have the same effect I did on Mom and bring her back. Their connection was so strong that she would want to engage with him. Every time he visited she would rally. At this point, her body was so shattered that it felt right to give her the space to let go. Kim stayed. We got everyone on the phone to say goodbye to her so she could hear their voice.

Kim was a rock for me during this final week. She slept on an air mattress on the floor a couple of nights in case Mom started to pass. On the days we stayed at my house, she got up with me early every morning so I didn't have to walk into the unknown alone. We alternated spending time with Mom so each of us could get some rest. I couldn't have asked for a better sister. She might have been my sister-in-law, but she was a sister to me in all ways that counted.

Loyce set up an appointment and brought me to the funeral home. There was no part of me that wanted to go, but we had to plan what would happen with Mom's body when she died. Loyce knew it would give me peace of mind to have arrangements made, which it did.

Mom wanted to be cremated and my brain connected to the words that the saleswoman was saying, but only just barely. Caskets, memorial, ashes, an urn. The words blurred in my mind. We figured out a plan so that I could call them anytime day or night when she died, and I left feeling nauseous and stunned. Reality is a beast at times.

For a week straight, Mom ate nothing, drank nothing, and breathed about five breaths per minute. She had cancer in her body and was dying, but she seemed to be waiting for something.

Kim and I continued to take turns being with her. We gave her space in case she needed to be alone to die. We did everything we could to keep her well medicated and comfortable, and she didn't die.

And she didn't die.

Friends came and went. We prayed over her and held space with her. She looked peaceful and she looked dead, but she still breathed.

The energy in the room was beautiful, and yet the human reality was so hard. As I sat with Mom, I felt her soul say to me, "Look to my spirit, not to my form." She was encouraging me to turn to the part of her that was eternal and to let go of focusing on her physical death. This is easier said than done. Her light was tangible in the room and the energy was rich with love, but her body looked like a breathing corpse.

We became friends with the nurses who were caring for her. There was so much love in all of our hearts, but there was also trauma and exhaustion in all of us who held the space with Mom.

Finally, I saw that there was going to be a full moon in a couple of days. On January 30th it was a blue moon, super moon, blood moon lunar eclipse, and the energy of the full moon was always a powerful thing for Mom. She was named Diana for the goddess of the hunt and of the moon. Her astrology sign was Cancer, and the ruling planet of Cancer is the moon.

I had a feeling that she was waiting for this auspicious lunar display. On the day of the full moon, all of her Albuquerque friends came to see her. We prayed over her and sang to her and loved on her and then we left to give her some space. Still she breathed.

I felt like I needed to leave so she could let go.

While I was gone, I was compelled to go looking for the spelling of her mom and dad's full names because we needed them for the death certificate.

I was rifling through Mom's important documents and came upon a piece of paper where she had written the date that both of her parents had died. I was dumbstruck.

My grandmother had died on the exact same date, January 30th, almost thirty years before. With the paper there was a handwritten note.

She sees her mother's humanness, her mom's heart. She sees that her mother is happy for her and wishes in her heart of hearts happiness for her mom as well.

It felt like a sign that Mom had resolved her fear about seeing my grandma, and I felt certain that Grandma was helping her to let go.

I went back to see Mom and told her that Grandma was with her. Kim, some friends, and I spent time with Mom and then went to dinner to give her space again in case she needed to be alone to pass.

When we went to the parking lot, the full moon was rising. There was a pink halo around it that was the exact color of Mom's hair. It was gigantic in the sky as it rose; New Mexico's moonrises are epic. We all paused and felt the glory of the moment.

We sat down for dinner and ordered food and a vodka gimlet to toast her.

During the toast, the music in the restaurant that had been quiet and unnoticeable started to make loud buzzing sounds like Mom's talker. It felt like Mom was calling us. *"It is time."*

We needed to go.

We paid the bill and hurried to the nursing home that was just two minutes away. As we drove, the moon had risen to its full glory.

We reached Mom's room right as she had taken her last breath. We could see that she had passed. I ran to her and felt, thump . . . thump . . . THUMP. Mom's last three heartbeats. And then she was gone.

She had called us back. She needed the space to go but gave me the gift of her last three heartbeats. I got to be with her when she passed.

There is no describing the emotional pain of actual death. She had looked dead for a while, but when a spirit leaves a body it is a whole different level of loss. A gaping abyss opened in my heart that felt like it could never heal. We all sobbed and prayed and said our goodbyes.

While I had said goodbye before, the last goodbye is the hardest, and all I could do was thank her for being the best friend and best mom. I had to let go of this beautiful human who had brought me life, and it will always make me cry to remember our final farewell.

You know when you get a form and it says,

"THIS PAGE IS INTENTIONALLY LEFT BLANK"?

This page represents the abyss that you feel after someone you love dies and is intentionally left blank.

From this page, I send you love and light.

Chapter Thirty-Six

Stopping and Restarting

Dear Friends,

Some of you may have heard that my beautiful mom, who I called Mamacita, passed away last night during the full moonrise. She had come to terms with dying in such a profound way, and up until the very last moment, the very last breath, she brought deep connection, love, and compassion to everyone around her. Her birth into spirit was in her own time and on her own terms, and I am so grateful and profoundly moved to have shared such a sacred moment with her.

Before she started actively dying, I asked her if she could be anywhere in the world where would she like to be. She looked me in the eyes and said, *"Right here."* What a lesson. To be fully content where we are, even when our surroundings and our life is so far from perfect. I know she is truly resting in peace.

She is with us all, lighting up our lives with inspiration, laughter, and a little bit of spice for eternity and beyond. I feel her so strongly that I know we get to begin a new conversation in our hearts. I will miss her physical presence dearly, but I will celebrate her in my life in every way I can. On the wings of Angels, Mamacita! Thank you all for your kind words.

Love and Light, Liz

L osing Mom crushed me. I knew she was alive in spirit, but I would never get to hear her laugh again, I would never get to hug her, and I would never get to hear her perspective on life in her voice.

I am someone who believes in a soul. I am someone who connects with those who have died, and I have had profound experiences that go beyond my logical mind and help me to feel and know that there is more to death than just an end. Even in the midst of this knowing, I had to feel the silence of Mom's physical death. And it was a deafening silence.

The morning after she died, a few of us woke up at dawn to see the lunar eclipse. We drove to the foothills with our Starbucks in honor of Mom and watched as the moon was covered in shadow. All of us were stunned and exhausted.

A lunar eclipse is an incredible symbol of death and grief. From the darkness, the moon emerges, but it is a slow progression and different light and nuances of illumination are created along the way.

Life eclipses death in the end.

The beauty and light of what was shared transcends the shadow and darkness of dying, death, and grief, but it is a painstakingly long process.

Kim and I drove to the Bosque del Apache that day, and we watched as thousands of snow geese flew over our heads. They looked like diamonds in the sky, and it felt like a salute to Mom. Kim flew home the following day, and I began the next step of my journey.

Grief.

Mom's Albuquerque crew went with me to the funeral home to say goodbye to her body. The final hurdle.

It no longer felt like her, and we honored her physical form one last time. Mike, Kim, the kids, and Aunt Betty had sent me notes, drawings, and flowers to place with her, which we did. Once they closed her cremation box, we adorned it with drawings of colorful dancers, all of her favorite animals, people, and places. Each of us wrote her a message of love and we left in tears. We sent her off to her next existence with style.

Part of being fully alive was to let myself mourn and feel the depth of emotion that came with the grieving process.

Because I was Mom's caregiver, my life for the previous five years had been filled with appointments, errands, life-threatening ailments, bucket lists, and so much more. Much of my life centered on caring for Mom. So, naturally, when she died, my life became very open.

Openness and time were things I craved dearly in the midst of Mom's trials. For five years, I felt like there was never enough time or energy to do everything I wanted to do.

Every moment with Mom had centered around the profound awareness of our mortality. Every choice had extra impact because it might be the last time Mom experienced something, and it might be the last time I got to experience something with her. There was a heightened awareness of life that made everything more poignant.

Also, every moment had centered around cancer and the treatment of a severe illness, which had constant twists and turns and curveballs. I couldn't really stop and rest when there was an awareness of a lurking beast ready to grab Mom's body and mind.

When Mom died, everything, all of that stopped.

She went off to a new realm, and I was left with nothing to do that had any type of meaning close to what she and I had experienced together. Plus, there was a deep hole that no one and nothing could fill. My mom, my confidant and my buddy, was no longer here.

The first few months for me were just a recovery from the strain of watching Mom die. The last two months of her life were filled with such traumas that I didn't even know I was grieving at first. Or maybe I should say that in the midst of grief, I was experiencing post-traumatic stress.

Being outside was the one thing that soothed my heart. Just seeing something beautiful helped me to remember the bigger picture of life. We are all just a small piece of something greater, and knowing that by witnessing nature helped me to heal.

I would force myself out of the house, and once I got out, the part of me that needed to experience the world came alive. Feeling alive helped me to know that eventually I would find my way through the heavy and intense emotions I was processing.

Being in the incredible landscapes of New Mexico was a life vest for me. Everyone has their own life vest: something that inspires or comforts the soul. For some it might be exercise, meditation, prayer, music, writing, dancing, art, watching movies, or talking to people. The activities I loved got me through the easy times with more joy, but they also saved me when I was facing grief.

The only way for me to heal was to walk head-on into my emotions while holding on to my life vests. I had many good cries in the mountains of Albuquerque.

After Mom died, life was filled with all of the exploring she and I would have done together. I learned that I could do the things she and I enjoyed doing either alone or with other people, but I missed her dearly.

Everyone who had gone through Mom's passing was going through their own grieving process. We were like the raccoons in Mom's story with her dad. Some of us ran around dazed, some of us clung to Mom's memories, and some of us cried out loud. Everyone grieves differently, and it was hard to know how to be there for each other.

For me, the best and most supportive thing that people did was to send love, to allow me not to be okay, and to just make sure I knew they were there.

I found myself talking to the most interesting people about grief and loss. One day, I was feeling acutely sad about Mom when I went to a party. There was a man who asked about how I was doing with the loss of Mom. He was someone I would not have expected to sit with and talk about death.

He and his wife had lost people and animals who were close to them. I could see in his eyes the understanding of the heartbreak that comes with death.

His wife came over and talked with me as well. We were able to go to a place in our hearts that was wounded and broken, and yet we were able to share it together from a space of love and compassion. It was very healing.

The fact that they were able to be present with me and ask questions and really listen was incredibly supportive.

What triggered grief for me often was so random that there was no way to predict it. A song on the radio, a person who looked like Mom on a trail, or a memory popping up in my mind could bring me to tears. There was no holding back the tears; they would be there before I even knew I was feeling something.

There were other times when the triggers were a little more understandable, even though they would still surprise me. Because Mom was dying over Christmas, the first time I saw Christmas lights the next year I could not stop crying. The year before, while everyone was celebrating the holidays, I was in the hospital watching my mom die. Christmas has an association that will take some time to heal.

There were many triggers like Christmas that stopped me in my tracks and helped me to feel and release emotions that had accumulated from daily living. There were many times I had to put my grief aside so that I could work, have relationships, and just function.

Since the triggers were unexpected, they were mostly unavoidable. They were much more frequent at the beginning of grief, and as the days unfolded, the triggers became fewer and farther between. Healing really does happen.

My goal after Mom died was to not fill my time; it was to really let life stop and in the stopping to let it reset. Throughout all of the years of helping people to heal from grief, I knew it would be tempting to make big changes in my life just to push away the grief and feel better for a moment. This can seem perfectly logical at the time, but it can create major problems in the future. So I sat with the discomfort of doing nothing.

The great element of sitting with nothingness was that life rose up from that nothingness to meet me. By letting myself sit still and feel the post-traumatic stress and the grief, I found that there was still life within me. It was buried at first under a lot of emotional rubble. Letting myself go through that rubble was a beast some days. I let myself not be okay, and by doing so I became more and more okay.

I felt my grief a lot in the middle of the night. I don't know if I would dream about Mom or if my subconscious was just active, but

I would wake up with a memory of something Mom and I did or something I went through during her dying process.

Usually tears just poured through me, and I let myself sit there with the sadness and memories until they were done. Eventually I was able to fall back asleep. The first year after Mom died, I slept very little. I have heard this is common.

Before Mom died, she and I got in the habit of telling each other that we would meet in our dreams. While she was sick, I talked with her on the phone every night before we went to sleep, and we would pick a place we wanted to go. New York City and Paris were our favorite choices, with Maui and Moab coming in close after that.

We wanted to practice connecting with each other in a more ethereal way, in our spirit and not just in person.

Occasionally one or the other of us would actually have a dream where we had planned to go. It always felt like a great success. We would call each other and say, "We did it! We made it to New York," and both of us would be so happy to know that it worked.

Now Mom comes into my dreams to help me to heal. I have had one or two New York City dreams and at least one Paris dream since she died. I wake up wanting to call her and tell her, "We did it!" but I have to just say it in my heart and trust that she knows it instead.

After time, I could feel the lessons I learned with Mom awaken in me.

I think of losing Mom as a part of me that is broken. Like a severely broken leg that never fully healed and gave me a limp. I can live with the pain. Sometimes it is severe and sometimes it is almost nonexistent. I can deal with it, because the "limp" has become a reminder of the love we shared.

I think of Mom and how she was broken in the end and how the broken parts made her better. Made her more grateful. Made her more alive. If she could have those enormous obstacles and still find inspiration to live, then my grief can do the same for me. It can teach me compassion and empathy, and it can ultimately wake me up to life.

Living with the knowledge of dying is such a profound place to live. Life lights up and has meaning in a way that makes every choice more significant. Appreciation is just a natural way of being, and it no longer takes conscious effort to create.

Losing Mom hurt, it sucked, it was devastating; there are no words, but it made me feel. It taught me to connect to life with a richness that I hadn't known existed. In this place I have found true gratitude.

Thank you, Mom. I miss you.

Chapter Thirty-Seven

The Unseen World

After Mom died I took a walk to pay tribute to her
on every full moon. There was a walk I did each
day on the last week of her life. It was in an area next to her nursing
home called Bear Canyon. That week, Kim and I would get to Mom
early in the morning to see if the nurses or doctors needed us. Once
we took care of the necessities for Mom, we would go for a hike in
Bear Canyon.

There was a statue of a bear mom with two cubs at the far end
of the canyon, and the round-trip trek to the statue was one hour. It
felt symbolic to take a pilgrimage to a bear mom and her two cubs
every day while Mom was dying. In my mind, Mom, my brother
and I were all depicted in the figures, and the strength of the bears
fueled me.

Someone placed painted rocks at the bear's feet that said things
like "love," "be strong," "be brave," and other encouragements. Before
Mom had been consumed by cancer, she and I had painted our own

rocks in similar fashions and left them around town, so it felt very soothing to have strangers doing the same for us.

After she passed away, on one of the full-moon walks in honor of Mom, I saw a bobcat.

Mom had a story she liked to tell about seeing a bobcat down by the river. She was with her dog Rosie, and the bobcat walked right in front of her. Rosie had been off leash, and Mom was able to grab her before she chased it. The bobcat flicked its tail at them and then disappeared into the bushes. The experience took Mom's breath away. She loved the majesty that she saw in the cat and told the exhilarating tale often.

In all of my years of hiking weekly and sometimes daily in Albuquerque, I had never seen a bobcat. I am certain that bobcats had seen me, but they had never shown themselves. When I looked up bobcat symbolism, many sources said that they symbolize something hidden in plain sight and that they teach us we are not alone. Spirit and our ancestors are with us.

After Mom died, I saw three bobcats within three months.

The first bobcat I saw I was with my brother. He came out to Albuquerque so we could have a memorial for Mom a couple of weeks after she died. She had wanted a hootenanny, which is a party with folk music and singing, so we had one and told stories of Mom, sang Lyle Lovette and Bob Dylan songs, and drank vodka gimlets in her honor.

I took Mike to the Bosque del Apache so he could see one of Mom's favorite places. It was mid-February and a little late in the season to see the sandhill cranes and snow geese, but we drove through the refuge anyway, and a bobcat came casually out of the bushes in front of our car, glanced at us, and sauntered across the road into the brush. It was unmistakable, beautiful and very close-up. What an incredible sight!

The next bobcat I encountered was the one I saw in Bear Canyon on my second full-moon walk. I had my two little dogs with me, and a big bobcat walked in front of me on the trail. It was about a block away. This was a bit more of an intense experience, like Mom and Rosie's, because I was fully exposed to the bobcat and not safely in a car. It casually looked at me, and then it strolled along the trail away from me, flicking its bobbed tail. The dogs were behind me and oblivious.

I watched it walk away and then turned in the other direction.

I spotted the third bobcat in the mountains next to my house. I decided to sit on a rock and contemplate life. After a while, I glimpsed movement nearby and a bobcat peeled itself off of the ground and started doing bobcat yoga. It was aware of me but not threatened, and the dogs and I made our way away from it slowly and respectfully. The dogs completely missed seeing this one as well, thank goodness. This last sighting demonstrated the symbolism of the bobcat so well. I was staring at the landscape and there was seemingly nothing there. By sitting still and just being, just observing, the landscape came alive, and something majestic revealed itself to me.

My feeling of connection with Mom is similar. I cannot feel her or know she is with me when I am active or my mind is occupied. I only feel her when I am still. In that stillness, her spirit comes alive and I feel her presence.

She rises to greet me in my heart and there I hear her voice.

She is here. She is with me.

Chapter Thirty-Eight

Memories Imprinted
on Our Heart

Think about the hundreds and thousands of hours of living that we forget about. There's no memory at a conscious level anyway. I simply can't remember how my family went about getting up and ready for the day, for instance. It's almost a complete blank. Sure, I can remember my dad standing before the bathroom mirror shaving and talking to himself. And I can see my mom's funny underpants. I can't really remember living in the bedroom downstairs in the house on Layton Avenue, just living in the upstairs bedroom where my sister and I moved later. Think of how many other instances like this that are lost to eternity.

I found the paragraph above worked into multiple documents of Mom's after she died. She had copied and pasted it into her novel and in many other files on her computer. It must have been something that she was contemplating at the end of her life.

Some of the memories I have with Mom awaken in my mind as I think about what she wrote.

When I was young, she read us chapters of *Watership Down*, by Richard Adams. It's a book about rabbits who have conversations, relationships, and adventures. Mike and I would bring our pillows and gather on either side of Mom on her big comfortable bed, and she would relate the tale with enthusiasm.

I never understood why we didn't finish the book, but found out later that I began to get upset with the story when the rabbits started dying. One of her favorite linguistic expressions in the book was when the rabbits would go out and "silflay in the grass," which basically meant they ate grass, but what a poetic word to use! I still remember how she played with the word "silflay" while she was reading the book to us. There was a feeling of complete safety and peace when my brother and I listened to Mom's lyrical voice filling our imagination with lively characters and scenes.

I can imagine her process when she realized the book was upsetting me and she needed to stop reading it. It must have been disappointing to her because I know she loved the time together as much as we did. She tried to taper off interest in the book by reading it less and less often, and I still can recall the feeling of sadness I had when we no longer read the book. I loved those rabbits and those sweet times with her.

First memories are intriguing.

My first memory was getting a real bed. I remember my dad putting it together and my mom putting on the sheets and blankets, and then I remember climbing into bed and feeling how big it was. I was lying on my bed stretching out and it was blissful.

My own first memory is so vivid, but I am not sure how real it is. I was in Mom's parents' car driving out West. My family and my grandparents had decided to go to Cooke City, Montana, so my grandpa could go fly fishing and we could explore the mountains. I got to be in my grandparents' car all by myself without my brother.

The smell of the leather in the car, the love from my grandparents, and the incredible views of plains and mountains fill my mind as I remember. There is a recollection of freedom, love, support, and happiness, and that is my full memory.

There's something about the feeling of being safe and loved that fills potentially mundane moments with more significance than meets the eye. I have had great and grand adventures, but I tend to feel more depth in the memories of small moments of connection with people in my life.

While first memories are significant, so are our final memories with people we love.

Right around the time I turned thirty-five, my father was diagnosed with prostate cancer. The outlook was not optimistic, and he had to go through a long series of radiation treatments and was in and out of the hospital for months and months. It was a difficult time for our whole family. For my sister and me, it was the first time in our lives that we were faced with losing someone so close and so important to us.

My father's condition worsened, and he was staying in a nursing home not far from my house. I tried to visit him every day. One night, I was at home after teaching all day and had just made dinner for my husband and two children.

I had planned to go and see my dad that night, but I decided I was just too tired.

I was going upstairs to change out of my work clothes when I got an overwhelming feeling that I needed to go and see my dad right then. I knew in my heart that he was going to pass away that night and he needed us by his side. Now at that time I was not religious and didn't have much of a spiritual life at all, but amazingly I listened to that feeling and sped over to the nursing home. Sure enough, my dad was failing fast and I called my mom and sister. Because of my heartfelt feeling, we all got to talk to my dad one last time, and were there with him when he passed away at about one in the morning.

And this amazing thing also happened when my mom died. She too was in a nursing home after she began to lapse into kidney failure. I was on my way to work and was planning to see my mom that evening. After making a turn toward work and away from the nursing home, I was engulfed by an urgency to see my mom. It was difficult at first to pay attention to this feeling since I had an important meeting in twenty minutes, but, without further hesitation, I made a U-turn and headed to see my mom. As I rushed down the hall to her room, a nurse caught sight of me and told me that my mom had taken a sudden turn for the worse just minutes before and she had been about to call me. I immediately called my sister and because of my "felt sense," we again were able to be with my mom when she passed.

I will never forget Mom calling me back to her side so I could be with her for her last heartbeats, the full moon bright and powerful in the sky, guiding her home.

Remembering Mom fills my heart with a deep feeling of love and acceptance. Her unconditional love is rooted in my soul. It is not just a memory; it is the truth of my relationship with her, and that truth will never die.

Chapter Thirty-Nine

X's on My Heart

I've always felt a great affinity for the moon. As an adult, I learned that the moon is the ruling planet of Cancer, my astrological sign, but all through my life I've often felt as if it were "speaking" to me. The full moon, especially in the New Mexico sky, often showed up at auspicious times in my life.

One night recently when I went out to take my dog Rosie for a walk, I came out of the gate of my house, and the whole sky was alive with the light of the full moon just rising over the Sandia Mountains. I kept getting glimpses of the moon during our walk as it flickered between the trees. For some reason, my thoughts turned to all the important healing work I had done in the past six months or so, and I felt gratified for that process. When I headed east to go home, there was the full moon again in all of its majesty, having risen high in the sky. I felt a chill throughout my body and I smiled.

And then the most amazing thing happened. I was immediately drawn to look just to the left of the moon and there before me was an enormous X in the universe, written, it seemed, by a cloud magic marker. It stretched across the entire sky, like nothing I had ever seen before, and I immediately knew that my angels were giving me a sign that, indeed, they were there for me, supporting and loving me. And then I remembered the mark our family always made when we signed our names on birthday cards, with an X for a kiss and an O around it for a hug.

I watched the X with amazement as Rosie and I walked the remaining few blocks home and, just when we reached our gate, the X seemed to suddenly "poof" from the sky, making its appearance seem all the more magical.

As the memories of Mom awakened inside me and helped me feel connected to her, I also started getting messages from Mom after she died.

During the times Mom and I talked about dying, we talked about how she would say hello and let me know that she was around once she passed. Her friend Mark showed her he was with her with yellow cars, and she wanted her own signature hello.

Mom always talked about the X's in the sky after her experience on her walk. The X's are the jet trails formed by airplanes crossing each other in the sky.

When we talked about how she would let me know that she was there, I suggested the X's because it was something I had never thought about before and not many people noticed or mentioned. It was unique to Mom, so it felt like a great way for her to say hello.

After she died, the sky was covered with X's on some of my hardest days of grief or on days that she would most want me to know she was with me. It's so interesting because there are days that go by where there are no X's. On certain days there are more X's than sky.

Recently, I was in Seattle with my niece and nephew on the first anniversary of Mom's death.

Mike and Kim were going on a trip during this time and asked me to take care of Chris and Abby while they were away. It was divine for me to get to spend this important day with two of Mom's favorite people, her grandkids.

The night before the anniversary of Mom's passing, I went to bed and something woke me out of a deep sleep. It seemed like I had seen lights going on and off, but I couldn't figure it out because I had been sound asleep. I got up to go to the bathroom, and while I was there, the light that I had left on as a nightlight started turning off, then on, then off for a while, and then on again. It didn't flicker, and it was turning off and on in no particular rhythm. I started laughing and said, "Hi Mom," and then it turned on and stopped turning off.

On January 30th, Chris and I told some stories about Mom, and then Abby and I went to lie down for the night. I had told them both about the light. Abby and I were remembering Mom and all of the good times we had with her. The light started turning off and on whenever she and I said something that felt meaningful. We laughed and said, "Hi Grandma."

Of course, as much as I believe in spirit and that Mom is with me, there is still a human part of me that doubts it now and again. I started thinking that my brother's light was defective and that was what caused the light trick.

The next night Chris camped out in the room with us to see if he could see the light, but we all fell asleep before it happened. We had consciously turned on the light that had been acting up. When

I got up that night to go to the bathroom, the light that had been going on and off was turned completely off. A different light had been switched on.

I couldn't wait to hear whether the kids had gotten up in the night to turn it on and they swore they didn't. They are deep sleepers, so I knew that they hadn't. Mom! She wanted to disprove my theory on the light going off because it was defective and she did a great job of showing us she was there.

What I have realized in this journey through grief and through all of the signs that Mom is with me, is that there is no way for her to leave me. She is integrated in my heart because we shared an unbreakable bond.

While I can't pick up the phone and talk to her anymore, and I can't give her a hug, I can still connect to the place where she resides in my heart. I can still find strength from the love and the laughter we shared. That place in me will never die.

Love shared never leaves us.

While it is so awesome and profound that Mom finds ways to say hello, the true connection with her is internal.

That doesn't mean I want her to stop lighting up the sky with as many X's as she can muster and saying hi to her grandkids in ways that will keep them laughing.

Here's Mom's recollection of her father visiting her after he died.

My dad had passed away in April, and that next Christmas my husband and I, my children, and my mother were in Phoenix, Arizona, visiting my husband's family. My father was on all of our minds during our stay since it was the first major holiday without him.

One night, a large group of us went to Pinnacle Peak, a steakhouse about an hour away in the mountains. It was one of our favorite haunts in Arizona and my parents had been there with us several times. It was a high-spirited, informal kind of place with just the kind of atmosphere my father liked. He always wore a tie there because he knew the waitress would march right over to him and ceremoniously cut it off with a humongous scissors and hang it up on the wall or the rafters to join the ties already there. And he always got a kick out of it because, when someone ordered a steak well done, they were served a hot, singed cowboy boot on their plate.

On this visit, I suddenly happened to look up at the bar that was off to our right, and there, sitting at the end and as full of life as he had ever been, was my dad. I knew right away that it was him. He wore his old tattered fishing hat and he was downing a shot of whiskey, and laughing at a joke from the bartender. I turned to my mom to tell her what I'd seen, but she was busy talking to my daughter. When I turned back to look again, my dad was gone, just like that. But, I know to this day that he indeed paid me a visit that night and gave me one last glimpse of him in all of his glory.

Chapter Forty

Mothers Are Embedded in Our Soul

Dear Liz,

This day has just begun. I'm sitting in my warm kitchen, looking out at the cold, still day, and I'm thinking about you.

I know this past year has been difficult for you, but it's been full of adventure and learning, too. You have good new friends; you wrote your best story yet. The most important part is that you've learned a lot about yourself, something some people never do.

A poem of mindfulness from Thich Nhat Hanh:

Peace is every step.
The shining red sun is my heart.
Each flower smiles with me.
How green, how fresh all that grows.
How cool the wind blows.

Peace is every step.
It turns the endless path to joy.

Love, Mom

Dear Liz, Thank you so much for everything you do for me—
calling me every day, making up all kinds of fun things to do,
and just being you. I'm so happy that you are my daughter
in this lifetime. You are an inspiration and bring me so much
joy. You brighten up my life each and every day. I love you,
Mamacita

As time has gone on and I have lived without Mom in this world, I have found myself observing mothers and daughters. What makes up this unique relationship for us? My mom and I were very close, but I know that is not true for a lot of people.

Regardless of closeness, a mother is an important relationship. She brings us our foundations for the life that we live here on earth. Most of us have to build our own new foundations, and some of us have to radically shift those foundations, but our moms create an initial space for us to observe the world.

I was recently at the airport sitting next to a young woman talking to her mom on the phone. I was eating my dinner as she was talking, and I heard her telling her mom about her new haircut. She went on to FaceTime to show off her new coif, and she had her phone on speaker so her whole conversation was loud and on display.

They spent a long time discussing her hairstyle, and I could tell the young woman wanted her mom's approval, which this particular mom did not give. Approval or not, the mom spent a long time on the phone with her daughter giving her attention and listening to her insecurities about her appearance.

While I was listening to them, I thought back to a time when my mom and I went shopping for new glasses for me. I unquestionably took for granted the fact that Mom was always willing to go on errands like this with me. We were looking through the glasses for a long time, and I finally found a pair I liked and showed them to Mom.

"They're alright . . . If you like that sort of thing," she said to me with a disdainful tone.

We both looked at each other and then burst out laughing.

I didn't buy the glasses and finally found some we both liked.

From then on, anytime one of us did not like something the other did, we would say, "It's alright . . . If you like that sort of thing."

In my relationship with Mom, we were able to laugh about a lot of things where other people might be insulted. I know some mothers and daughters can relate and some are the exact opposite. Some moms and daughters feel hurt and insulted by each other all the time.

Recently I was in an airplane with open seating, and I saw a mom tell her husband she was going to sit with their daughter instead of him. You could hear him grumbling about it. It turned out to be a brave choice on the mom's part because she sat right behind me, and I heard the loud conversation between the mom and daughter.

The mom was gently asking the daughter about a guy the daughter liked. The daughter started in on the mom, saying she didn't want to talk about it and how dare the mom bring it up. Then the daughter started loudly complaining that her cell phone was out of batteries and she couldn't listen to her music.

The whole time, the mom was present with her daughter even though there was constant berating and complaining from the daughter. The mom stuck it out and held space for the daughter to be in an awful mood. I tuned them out and fell asleep, but I noticed at the end of the trip, the daughter was smiling and laughing with her mom and they both looked so content and happy. The mom had healed her daughter's bad mood and the daughter didn't even know it.

I would love to say that I was never that daughter, but of course I was at times. Some moms are remarkable for their ability to love, no matter what. Mine was definitely that way.

On one occasion, Mom was helping me move apartments. I was living in a place up in the mountains and had to take the trash to the dump because there was no trash pickup. I remember being in a huge hurry. I was bugged with my mom because she was dawdling. I tore out of the driveway and drove off angrily.

Mom bravely called me later and heard me bickering about all the things that I had to do. Somehow, with her Mom magic, she helped me shift gears so that by the end of the conversation we were laughing about the way I had peeled out of the driveway with wild abandon.

Mothers can be such powerful healers, and they heal while getting very little recognition.

I never realized fully how Mom was able to hear me. She knew me so well and knew how to hold space for me to work through things.

I want to tell the daughters that I see how lucky they are to have their mom. To be able to talk to them. To be able to hug them. To be able to be in a bad mood with them. To be able to be in a good mood with them. To be healed by them without even knowing it's happening.

The biggest thing I've noticed as time goes on without Mom here is the loss of a loving witness. Mom was there for me in all my highs and lows. I was there with her for all of her highs and lows as I became an adult.

I know Mom is still loving me and witnessing me from spirit, and yet there is a deep loss in not being able to call her up and talk with her about the good, the bad, and the ugly in life. I miss having her here to listen for hours as I worked through issues, and I miss listening to her for hours as she worked through problems as well.

I know this has been a rough year for our whole family, and I wanted you to know how much I appreciate all the ways you have helped me through it. I love you more than I can say.

That presence of a person who knows all of your good, and puts up with all of your underbelly, is invaluable in life.

For some people, that loving witness is a friend, a romantic partner, a father, a sibling; but for me it was my mom.

Chapter Forty-One

A Story Left Mid-sentence

New Mexico is filled with ghost towns like the one my family and I went to with Mom. Some of them have communities living there again and some of them are completely deserted.

When I was in my twenties, I explored a ghost town that looked like it had been abandoned in the middle of a meal. Tables were set, newspapers were out, and it appeared like people had just gotten up and left in mid-sentence. This always stuck with me and felt bizarre.

When Mom died, there was that same feeling. Yes, she knew she was going to die, but while she was dying she kept on living.

When she left her house for the last time, there were groceries in her refrigerator ready to eat, there were plans she had with friends, email and text conversations with people, bills to be paid, doctor's appointments, and a half-written novel on her desk. There was life left in the future that wouldn't be lived.

While it took Mom two months after leaving her apartment to pass away, for me there was the constant need to face a life that was ending on the physical level but that was still alive in front of me.

When Mom was dying she had a studio apartment in her independent living facility that was three-hundred square feet. All of her life and personality was in that room with her. There were eclectic paintings on the wall, and she had Buddhas and storyteller dolls placed around the room. Her favorite painting at the end of her life was an abstract forest scene that had cheerful colors and hung over her bed.

Mom was an artist and loved to paint, so there were acrylics out, and a half-painted birdhouse was sitting on her art table ready to be finished.

When it was clear that Mom would not make it home, it was emotional to break her house down. What to keep, what to donate, what to give to friends and family, and how to mourn it all became a bit overwhelming.

The most unusual emotion that lingers even now is the feeling that life was left mid-sentence. Where would we be if, on that fated day that her cancer took her, she got up instead and had a regular day? If she was alive today, would she have finished her novel? Would the birdhouse be painted and hanging on her porch? Would we be on a road trip to Santa Fe drinking cappuccinos and daydreaming together?

Who can say? There will always be a stopping point in life, and it is surreal when we meet it.

We are human beings with potential until the day that we die. When we die, all of the physical potential we have stops.

We leave behind the impression of who we were.

Even when the things are cleaned up and sorted and the home is cleared, our essence, our purpose, is etched on everyone we knew and loved, just like the petroglyphs Mom and I saw in Utah.

That etching becomes potential in the people that we leave behind. I feel Mom alive in my heart in so many ways and I feel her presence. I feel her with me while I am writing this.

So, if she's here, what is she doing? If she left life in mid-sentence, then it would follow that she is still in the process of finishing her sentences.

My way of inquiring when it comes to the unseen world is to turn within. I can hear the subtle voice of spirit by stopping and listening. I quiet my mind and ask for a connection to the eternal energy of Diana Bee Steffen's soul.

When I ask in my heart what she's up to, I immediately get the message, *"No good!"* which of course helps me know that it's Mom. She loves to joke around.

So, I ask again, and she shows me an energy of love. There's a bit of a block for us to truly understand what comes next. We can't see it fully because if we did we would lose focus on where we are now, and where we are now is beautiful.

"It's beautiful where I am, but don't hurry here," I feel Mom say. "Live your life on earth. Enjoy being human. Make mistakes, love a lot, be yourself, and embrace that self. There's plenty of time to experience heaven. Life is but a blink of an eye. Dig into relationships. Breathe the fresh air. Eat good food. Savor the flavors. Get your body strong and feel the strength. Laugh at your personality. Connect with the divine. Have faith that there is more to it all, but enjoy the drama of being human and have a sense of humor about it. The end of life sneaks up on you, so enjoy all that you can."

A glimpse of Mom helps me to remember that, while her physical life is over, her spirit is eternal. The sentences that she didn't finish here on earth, I can support her in finishing. Or they can be let go.

I painted her birdhouse.

I ate her groceries, connected with her friends, canceled her doctor's appointments, paid her bills, moved some of her stuff to my house, and donated the rest of it to thrift stores.

I started to finish her book, but wrote this one instead.

I connect with Mom's spirit and soul often so that we can continue our journey, and I pay tribute to her by living my life as grandly as I can.

"Celebrate me through living, there's no better life than this one. The one that you are in right now. Whether you are happy or are sad. Whether you are healthy or unwell. Whether you are lonely or surrounded by love. You are ALIVE. And alive is enough to find something in your life that you love. It could be a person, an animal, a piece of art, a smile. It doesn't have to be anything big. Pick something that you love and then pick again. Soon your life will be lit up with things that you love. Gently let go of the things you don't love. When you choose love, life becomes alive. When you live life from simply being alive, it gets really good. Trust me, I know."

Just as the people in the ghost town moved out and led new lives somewhere else, Mom is off leading her new life in spirit with as much light as she did here on earth. I will see her again.

But for now, I can celebrate her by being ALIVE.

Chapter Forty-Two

Epilogue

A very meaningful connection with the world has emerged for me as I have walked my path and lived my life in the wake of Mom's passing. There are other people out there who have lost their parents or lost someone significant to them. An obvious statement, I realize, but it is such a relief to know.

It seems like loss draws us together, and it is something I feel intuitively when I meet someone.

So many times, I will mention a tattoo or a hair color and someone will say that they dyed their hair in memory of their mom or they got a tattoo in memory of a lost child or a father.

My hair has been many colors since Mom died, but it has been pink as a tribute to her more often than not. I got a tattoo of two sandhill cranes and the moon in honor of her.

If we pay attention, we see the signs of something significant that represents some*one* significant.

I have had such incredible connections with waiters, waitresses, cashiers, hikers, and people from every walk of life when I notice something, and they tell me about the important person they lost.

I recently found a sign at a flea market that said, "I love you to the moon and back," which was something that Mom said to me and reminded me of her.

When I went to the cash register to pay for it, the cashier told me she liked the sign and I said it reminded me of my mom.

"Is your mom still with you?" she asked.

"No, I lost her a couple of years ago," I said.

She got tears in her eyes and told me she had lost her mom on Thanksgiving the year before. The story was heart-wrenching. I listened and said I was so sorry.

My change from my purchase had been a penny, and I was holding it and wondering if there was a penny jar.

"My mom always says hello by showing me pennies," she said.

I held out the penny and said, "This is from your mom."

Her eyes filled with tears and she came around the counter and gave me a hug.

"You made my day," she told me.

"You made mine," I said.

We said goodbye from a deep place of connection and knowing.

Understanding profound loss is hard, but also such a gift. I can connect with people from a place that I never knew as thoroughly as I know now. I am so grateful for the stories that I hear.

We all have gone through loss. We all will go through loss.

And life eclipses death in the end.

Acknowledgments

When I finished the first draft of my book, I was perplexed. My mom was my editor throughout my life, so who could I show my writing to? Who would I trust to read and edit such a personal story? My good friend Gilden, who knew Mom and who is an incredible writer, came to my heart and mind and she agreed to edit it. She was the ideal first reader. She gave suggestions with kindness and compassion, and she stuck with me throughout all of my edits. My friend Julie, also a superb writer, came next and she helped me to identify and establish the story more clearly. Annie, Jan, Loyce, Terri, Kim, Mike, Aunt Linda, Aunt Betty, and my dad were great readers as well, and they each gave me solid feedback.

I am grateful beyond measure to all of my friends and family who stood by me before and after Mom died. Without my awesome people, I wouldn't be where I am now. Mom also had many friends who wrote to her and talked with her throughout her life and during her journey with cancer. I want to thank them for their amazing support, and I know she is with them lighting up their hearts with gratitude. Much love to you all.

About the Author

Liz Vance has a BA in Communications from the University of Wisconsin-Madison. At twenty-four, she was struck by lightning, and this life-altering event led her to become an intuitive life coach and healer for people across the globe. She teaches intuition and Reiki, writes blogs and newsletters, and creates online classes and videos. Her work centers around supporting people to live inspired lives, heal from grief, find their life's purpose, transform dysfunctional relationships, own their uniqueness, and love themselves more.  Her goal is to encourage people to live epic lives, and her website, www.theawakeself.com, offers tools to expand people's awareness of their inner wisdom and inner healer.

Diana Steffen always said writing was her middle name. Not only was she born to be a writer, but she also loved to inspire others to tell their stories. She taught writing and journalism at the high school and college level, and was an assistant director of marketing and a director of community outreach for Wisconsin Public Television. She had master's degrees in both English and Education from the University of Wisconsin-Madison. At the end of her life she tutored students and created solid foundations for them to write their way through life. Now she shines brightly in the hearts of all who loved her and learned from her.